Is
Christianity
True?

Is Christianity True?

Hugo A. Meynell

GEOFFREY CHAPMAN

Geoffrey Chapman
A Cassell imprint
Villiers House, 41/47 Strand,
London WC2N 5JE

First published 1994

British Library Cataloguing-in-Publication Data
A catalogue record for this book is available from the British
Library.

ISBN 0–225–66741-X

Phototypeset by Intype, London
Printed and bound in Great Britain by
Mackays of Chatham PLC

Contents

Acknowledgements

Parts of Chapter 1 have appeared in *The Month* and in *Proceedings of the Aristotelian Society*; and earlier drafts of Chapters 3 and 5 in *Theology*. A version of Chapter 2 originally appeared in *Religious Studies*. The material is printed here by kind permission of the editors of these journals. My thanks are also due to Avril Dyson for putting the text onto a wordprocessor, and to Irene Hergert and Perlea Ashton for revising it.

To Bat-Dimyon

Introduction

This book is addressed mainly to persons of good will who think that there may be something of value in Christianity, but that there are decisive intellectual and moral grounds for believing that it is not true.

What I shall try to show is that the Christian has good reason for believing what she characteristically believes. While some people object to this procedure on principle, I have never understood their objections. If anyone does not maintain that her own beliefs are rationally defensible, she is dishonest. If she thinks that they are not only rationally defensible, but of some importance and value, she will be blameworthy if she does not try to show their reasonableness and value to others.

It has been held in some quarters that one may brush aside all the arguments which have been brought against Christianity, if one takes it as a subjective stance towards the world and human life, without factual content. I believe that this kind of 'Christianity' is more or less worthless; but do not intend to go into the matter here.[1] I shall take for granted what has been assumed by nearly everyone everywhere since Christianity first came into the world: that it is committed to belief in certain matters of fact, and stands or falls with them.

My main concern in this little book will not be with what is for many people the crucial issue, belief that there is a God, because I think that it requires separate and extended treatment, and have provided it elsewhere.[2] But since the existence of God is after all a necessary presupposition of the truth of Christianity, it seems worthwhile for me to give a sketch in the present context of what I regard as the good reasons for believing in the doctrine. One may usefully distinguish between two sorts of atheism, which I shall label existential and theoretical. The existential atheist harps on the impairment and impoverishment of human life which seem to her part and parcel of belief in God. There can be no reasonable doubt, I'm afraid, that belief in God in general, and Christian belief in particular, has often been used as a means of keeping people in a state of deprivation, ignorance or infantilism. The crucial question is whether this is an abuse of theism and of Christianity which is no part of their essential nature, or whether it is a natural and inevitable consequence of them, as was maintained notoriously by Karl Marx and Friedrich Nietzsche. Certainly, the theist and Christian ought incidentally to argue against the existential atheist; but the principal appropriate response to such a person is to listen with the closest attention and respect to what she has to say, and to exert oneself to the uttermost to ensure that her reproaches should in future be deserved as little as possible.

The theoretical atheist characteristically holds that there is no good reason for believing that there is a God, and plenty of reason for maintaining that there is not. The proper response to the theoretical atheist is calmly and respectfully to refute her; that is, to show that her arguments are unsound, and that at least some of the arguments for theism are sound. (It should be noted that I am using the word 'refute' in the proper and not the debased and vulgar sense, in which 'to refute' means no more than 'emphatically to contradict'.)

It is sometimes maintained that it is proper to believe in God simply as a matter of faith, without or even in despite of any reasoning which is independent of such faith.[3] Closely related to this view is the position, ably defended by some contemporary thinkers, that belief that there is a God is a 'properly basic belief', that is, one that is and ought to be held without being justified by reference to any other belief.[4] After all, it is urged, not all our beliefs can possibly be justified by reference to other beliefs, or we would inevitably be involved in infinite regress. And if at least some of our beliefs must be basic in the sense that they cannot be thus justified, why should not belief in God be so? The principal objection to this view is just that, if belief in God is to be accepted as a properly basic belief, there seems no reason why any other belief, however absurd or monstrous it may seem to us, should not be accorded the same status by someone who is determined to maintain it. Why should not the flatness of the earth, or the bodily assumption of the late Joseph Stalin into heaven, or the appropriateness of burning to death lonely old people who own black cats, equally be defended as a 'properly basic belief'? It will be objected at this point that there is no overall means of determining which beliefs are rational, and which are not. But this seems to me simply false. In the case of any belief whatever, including that in the existence of a God, we may properly ask 'What is the evidence for it? Is it stronger than the evidence for its contradictory?' If the evidence against the existence of God turns out to be stronger than the evidence for it, then we ought to abandon that belief. Unless we hold fast to this principle, we might as well abandon ourselves once and for all to irrationalism.[5]

I believe that the most cogent reason for believing in the existence of a God is the openness of the universe to investigation by the human mind. Rationality is not merely a game which the human subject plays with herself; it is the means, and the only means, by which the deepest secrets of the material universe can be brought to light. If mind were a mere chance by-product of the endless movement of utterly mindless matter and energy, it is difficult to see how it could have this curious relationship

3

which it has to the cosmic order at large. In fact the whole scientific enterprise, which is so often believed to be intrinsically hostile, or at best indifferent, to belief in God, depends on the assumption of the universe's rationality, its susceptibility to explanation in terms of laws which can be grasped by the human mind. As C. S. Lewis put it, science is committed to the assumption that reality in its remotest nebula obeys the thought-laws of the scientist in her laboratory here on earth.[6] And the best explanation of the universe's having this nature and structure, such that it is intelligible and able to be compassed by inquiring minds, is that it is itself due to mind. By 'God' is generally meant the intelligent will supposed to give rise to the universe; the divine intelligence accounting for the fact that it is intelligible at all, the divine will for the fact that it has the particular sort of intelligibility that it has—in terms, so far as scientists know now, of hydrogen rather than caloric, of special relativity rather than a luminiferous aether, of evolution of species by mutation and natural selection rather than of special creation, and so on.[7]

The opponents of rational theism, whether they are atheists on the one hand, or people who would have the existence of God to be a matter of pure faith on the other, often appeal to the work of the philosophers David Hume and Immanuel Kant, as having shown once and for all that none of the arguments for the existence of God will work. But it is remarkable that the philosophical principles of both these thinkers, while issuing in radical objections to theoretical[8] arguments for the existence of God, also raise apparently insuperable difficulties in the way of human beings actually getting to know about the real world. (Hume is driven to the conclusion that, while virtually all our knowledge depends on the assumption of the existence of a causal nexus within the world, belief in such a causal nexus is itself founded on nothing more secure than our mental habits.[9] Kant is of the opinion that knowledge is rather a matter of imposing the structure of our minds upon phenomena, than of discovery within phenomena of structures answering those proposed by our minds; due to this limitation, as he sees it, knowledge of things as they are in themselves is impossible for us.[10]) Both philosophers are thus in their way witnesses to the fact that theism on the one hand, and that assumption as to the intelligibility and knowability of the real world on which science as usually understood depends on the other, in the last analysis stand or fall together.

It may be protested that the intelligibility of the universe is really to be explained in evolutionary terms.[11] The survival of organisms, it is said, and their ability to leave offspring, will plainly be greatly enhanced if they can get to understand and know about their environment. Given appropriate circumstances for the emergence and continuation of life, intelligent life was thus liable in the long run to evolve. The trouble with this supposed explanation, I believe, is that it puts the cart before the horse. I will concede for the sake of argument that, *given* an intelligible universe, creatures which were able to get to understand it would be liable in the long run to evolve in it. But this does not at all explain how the universe was intelligible *in the first place*—how it has always been such that finite minds such as ours, once they evolved, could come to understand it.

Two subsidiary arguments for the existence of God are worthy of mention. The great medieval Muslim theologian Al Ghazzali argued that anything which had not always existed requires a cause for its existence, and that the world could not always have existed; so a cause is required for the world's existence, and this is God. Al Ghazzali's reasons for believing that the world has not always existed, though ingenious and intriguing, do not convince me;[12] but twentieth-century science has apparently supplied another kind of support for the thesis. Soon after Einstein propounded his General Theory of Relativity, it began to appear both from theoretical con-

5

siderations and from observation that we live in an expanding universe; according to contemporary cosmologists, this must have originated in a single point-instant between fifteen and twenty thousand million years ago.[13]

It is commonly supposed that Charles Darwin administered the *coup de grâce* to the ancient argument to a divine Designer from the order in the universe. Darwin showed in principle how the elaborate structures of living beings might have come into existence over an enormous time by random mutations and natural selection, with organisms which failed to 'fit' their environment perishing without offspring; at this rate no designer would be needed. But recent cosmologists have pointed out that there appears to be a remarkable degree of 'fine tuning' towards the development of life in the laws and initial conditions underlying the universe. To take one example among several (I quote John Leslie), 'a reduction (of the expansion of the universe) by one part in a million at an initial stage would have led to recollapse before temperatures could fall below ten thousand degrees. An early increase by one part in a million would have prevented the growth of galaxies, stars and planets.'[14]

Some have actually argued that there must be billions of 'universes', for it not to be prohibitively improbable that this universe of ours should have come into existence by chance. (If the proverbial team of monkeys strumming on typewriters duly produce their Hamlet, one can be pretty sure either that the team is very large, or that their proceedings have been protracted over a very long period.) If this is really the alternative, design by an intelligent being could well recommend itself on grounds of economy. As the famous astronomer Fred Hoyle has put it, the universe shows definite signs of being a put-up job.

Against all such arguments to the existence of a God, the objection is often made that it makes no sense to appeal to what is somehow 'outside' or 'other than' the universe in purporting to explain it or some aspect of it.[15] The reason given for this is that the term 'the universe' *means* the sum total of what exists; so necessarily there cannot exist anything that is other than the universe itself or a part of it. I concede that, *if the universe is really the sum total of what exists,* then God, if God exists, must be a part of the universe, and so cannot be invoked as something 'outside' the universe to explain the existence of the universe or some aspect of it. But the qualification is crucial. In effect, to define 'the universe' in this way, and to claim that God is other than the universe or a part of it, is to assume from the outset that God does not exist. But if one is honestly and clear-sightedly to confront the question of whether there is reason to suppose that God exists, it seems wrong to presuppose either that God exists or that God does not exist. If one defines 'the universe' in the sense given, then the question to ask is: 'Within the universe, as the sum total of what exists, is it reasonable to suppose that there is some entity which is related to *the rest of* what exists rather as cause to effect, or as agent to the result of her action?' The arguments which I have outlined, I believe, do support the view that such an entity does indeed exist.

A closely-related objection runs as follows. Why should not the existence of the universe itself just be a brute fact? And if one objects to brute facts, doesn't the God invoked to explain the universe have to be just as much of a brute fact as would be the universe without such a postulated explanation? In general, it may be commented that the whole scientific enterprise seems to depend on the assumption that there are no brute facts; that things, events and states of affairs are all subject to explanation. If a supposed thing, event or state of affairs persistently refused to fit into any pattern of explanation, would this not be excellent reason for denying its reality?[16] As to the particular case of God, I do not think that the existence of a being that understands and wills all else that exists is 'brute' in the objectionable sense. Such a being, given that it existed at all, could not be due to anything else, or it would not be that on which *all else* (i.e. 'the universe' in the sense of all that exists which is other than God, in the case that God exists) depends for its existence. A brute fact in the objectionable sense is one that, while it might conceivably be subject to explanation, just happens not to be, and for no reason.

I am of course aware of many other objections which can be raised against each of these arguments. But I believe that all of them can be effectively answered, though I have no space to show this here.[17]

Probably the most serious ground for atheism is constituted by the reality of evil.[18] Here above all one must insist that the view of the atheist should be treated with the greatest respect and understanding; slickness or bluster about the matter by theists is inexcusable. God is supposed to be all-powerful and utterly good, yet the world which God is supposed to have created is full of intense pain and suffering, much of which it is absurd to attribute to the abuse of human free-will; how could such a God bring about, or even allow, this state of affairs? What may be called the 'classical' solution set out by Thomas Aquinas[19] still seems to me to provide the outline of what is the best approach to the matter for theists— that physical evil in any part of the universe is explicable in terms of the order of the whole; and that moral evil is permitted because it is better that there should be creatures like ourselves, with a real ability to choose between right and wrong, than that there should not be. And the moral excellence available to these creatures with the help of divine grace involves the overcoming of both physical and moral evil. If there is reason to suppose that there is intelligent agency at the base of the universe, this may provide some grounds for hope that there will ultimately be a universal consummation which will make all the agony appear worthwhile. Theists characteristically believe in special revelations by God, including the Christian one, which state specifically that such a consummation will in fact take place. The prospect of some form of life after death for human beings is, of course, a necessary condition for such a consummation; a curious feature of the present time is that, quite apart from the doctrines of the great religions, evidence for the reality of such a life after death appears to be steadily mounting, as I shall argue below.

The question I am concerned with in this book is this: in case there is a God, what reasons are there for thinking that Christianity is true, and so for being a Christian?[20] I shall begin each chapter with a question from an imaginary objector, which will set the agenda for discussion.

Notes

1 I tried to show this at some length in *Sense, Nonsense and Christianity* (London, 1964) and *The New Theology and Modern Theologians* (London, 1967).

2 See Hugo Meynell, *The Intelligible Universe* (London and New York, 1982).

3 See especially S. Kierkegaard, *Philosophical Fragments* (Princeton, NJ, 1962); K. Barth, *Church Dogmatics* (Edinburgh, 1936–64).

4 Thus A. Plantinga, 'Rationality and religious belief' in *Contemporary Philosophy of Religion*, ed. S. M. Cahn and D. Shatz (New York, 1982). A rather similar view is defended by N. Wolterstorff, *Reason Within the Limits of Religion* (Grand Rapids, 1984). For a critical discussion of these views, see Hugo Meynell, 'Faith, foundationalism, and Wolterstorff' in *Rational Faith*, ed. L. Zagzebski (Notre Dame, IN, 1993).

5 Someone who is philosophically inclined may ask: what is the status of the belief, that one should always believe propositions for which the evidence is stronger than for their contradictories? The answer is: that the contradictory of this belief destroys itself. Suppose someone asserts this contradictory. Either she asserts it because she has evidence for it, or she does not. If she does, she is committing herself after all to the principle that one should always hold beliefs for which the evidence

is stronger than for their contradictories. If she does not, what is the point of paying attention to her? Why take seriously anyone who advances beliefs for which she herself admits that she has no reason?

6 C. S. Lewis, *They Asked For A Paper* (London, 1962), p. 162.

7 The most thorough exposition of this argument known to me is to be found in chapter XIX of Bernard Lonergan, *Insight: A Study of Human Understanding* (Toronto, 1992). For a brief version, see R. Taylor, *Metaphysics* (Englewood Cliffs, NJ, 1963), pp. 98–101.

8 Kant thought that all alleged theoretical *disproofs* of God's existence were as fallacious as the alleged theoretical *proofs*; and that one ought to believe in God on the practical grounds that this was best for morality. See S. Körner, *Kant* (Harmondsworth, 1955), pp. 166–8.

9 See David Hume, *An Enquiry Concerning Human Understanding*, sections III-V, VII.

10 See Immanuel Kant, *Critique of Pure Reason*, Introduction to the second edition.

11 See Harry V. Stopes-Roe, 'The intelligibility of the universe' in *Reason and Religion*, ed. Stuart C. Brown (Ithaca and London, 1977).

12 In brief, his argument is that if the world had always existed, the past would consist of an infinite time. But if that were the case, since an infinite time can never elapse, we would not have got up to the present, which quite plainly we have. Therefore the world cannot always have existed, and so must have come into existence.

13 For a brilliant and comprehensive exposition and defence of this argument, see William Lane Craig, *The Kalam Cosmological Argument* (London, 1979). Of the great medieval Christian systematic theologians, it is notable that while Bonaventure accepted the argument as sound, Aquinas rejected it.

14 John Leslie, 'Anthropic principle, world-order, design', *American Philosophical Quarterly* (April 1982). The matter is also discussed at length in the same author's *Universes* (New York and London, 1989).

15 For a characteristically trenchant expression of this argument, see A. G. N. Flew, *God and Philosophy* (London,

1966), 3.15–16. Flew's book as a whole is a very useful exposition of the main arguments for atheism.

16 This does not really impugn the possibility of miracles, which, as I have argued elsewhere, are better thought of as events which are subject to explanation of a particular kind than as events which are absolutely inexplicable. See Hugo A. Meynell, *God and the World* (London, 1971), chapter 4.

17 See Meynell, *The Intelligible Universe*, passim.

18 For a more extended discussion of the matters dealt with in this paragraph, see Meynell, *God and the World*, chapter 3.

19 See Thomas Aquinas, *Summa Theologica* I, xlviii.

20 Some contemporary apologists base their case squarely on the historical evidence for the resurrection of Jesus: cf. Gary R. Habermas, *The Resurrection of Jesus* (Grand Rapids, 1980). I would regard this approach as complementary to the one followed here.

O N E

Isn't secular morality enough?

Author's note: The last half of this chapter is unavoidably somewhat technical. If the reader is unduly discouraged at this point, she should skip straight to Chapter 2.

'Even if there are good reasons for thinking that there is a God of the kind believed in by Christians, is not the worship of such a being at best morally irrelevant, at worst morally harmful?'

That we urgently need some moral principles, whether we are secularists or religious believers or undecided about the matter, is perhaps obvious to anyone with eyes in her head. Especially at a time of unprecedented environmental and social change, we need to have some idea of what goals are worth seeking, and why; and, among the goals which are worth seeking, which are practicable, and how. Inevitably, technological innovations and human injustices, especially between rich and poor countries, being what they are, we must change, and change fast; what we desperately need to know is which kinds of change would be desirable, which deplorable and even catastrophic. Short of this, either apathy and despair, or cynicism and self-seeking, would seem to be more or less inevitable.

Not only does the sheer rate of change make the need particularly acute at the moment; but there is abroad a rather widespread dissatisfaction with the values which once seemed to give some kind of overall direction to the activities of individuals and groups. Reasonably or otherwise, rather a lot of people have the uneasy feeling that neither the Western paradise of consumer goods nor the Marxist revolution has quite fulfilled their promises. Even if we had the resources to keep it up, which clearly we haven't, it would be generally agreed that the Western way of life does leave something to be desired.[1] Lucien Goldmann, himself a Marxist, compared Pascal's wager that Christianity is true with the Marxist conviction that a better world would arise as a result of the proletarian revolution.[2] More cynical students of twentieth-century history might say that where the bet has been made, the money has usually been lost. Christians feel that they ought to have something distinctive and useful to contribute. But how could such a contribution be of any significance to those who do not share Christian premises? And is it not rather unreasonable to suppose that Christianity might have a bearing on distinctively modern problems, when it came into the world so many centuries before they existed?

It appears to me that the material for a comprehensively critical social ethic, in which religion in general and Christianity in particular have an indispensable role to play, is ready to hand, but not yet properly co-ordinated. The reasons for the lack of co-ordination are various, and some of them will be mentioned incidentally in what follows.

Very roughly, the human good consists in the first place in the meeting of two sorts of need, material and social. Each person needs to be adequately fed, clothed, and housed, and wants to have other requisites for the relief of her pain and for her comfort and delight. She also needs the company and some measure of the affection of other persons. In a study of factors tending to lead to social breakdown, Eugene Heimler noted five main areas of life in which persons could find more or less satisfaction—financial, sexual, through family relationships, through friendship, and through work and interests.[3]

Now it is obvious that technological developments in modern times make an enormous contribution to the material aspect of the good of human beings. Their effect on the social aspect is a good deal more questionable. Co-operation in productive industry, as Marx and others have noted, can be a source of tremendous fellow-feeling in performance and achievement. On the other hand, the requirements of efficiency in production are liable to divide families and neighbourhoods, and the competition which it can engender corrupts and embitters human relationships in other ways. Also, of course, there are apt to arise gross injustices in the production and consumption of material goods, one class doing nearly all the latter, owning and controlling the means of production as it does, the other (the oppressed majority) doing nearly all the former. Similar relationships of domination and subjection may arise between countries as well as between classes within each country.[4]

Apart from these material and social facets, the human good has another and crucial aspect, which is a more or less necessary condition for gaining the rest. On what benefits the group as opposed to the individual, the wider community as opposed to the group, humankind at large as opposed to the wider community, people of the future as opposed to people of the present, one may be merely ignorant. But far more important, one may have motives for remaining ignorant, or even for increasing one's ignorance. Where my own self-interest, or that of my group, is in opposition to the general interest, I may attend very selectively if at all to the evidence bearing on the matter; I may more or less deliberately fail to envisage possible explanations of this evidence which are inconvenient; or if I envisage them, I may not sufficiently ponder whether they meet the evidence better than possibilities less irksome to me on the grounds of my prospects or my self-esteem. The counteracting of such tendencies to self-deception is among the most important of all factors contributing to the human good.

14

Few individuals or interest-groups have the perverse moral courage to act selfishly with full consciousness of what they are up to. A measure of self-deception, in other words, is necessary to life in the world if one is neither very good nor very bad. However, even self-deception has its price. The pathological effects in the individual which result from such restrictions in consciousness have been described in detail by Freud and his followers, those in the wider society by the Marxists. A person may be said to be in the grip of 'ideology' so far as she does not attend to evidence which might adversely affect her individual or class interests; or does not ask relevant questions about it, or judge or decide to act accordingly. An irascible or profligate husband and father, who makes the life of his wife and children a misery, is apt somehow not to attend to the evidence, or envisage the possibilities, which would lead to the judgement that they are unhappy because of the way in which he behaves, or to the decision to change it at some inconvenience to himself. Again, a class or group which lives at the expense of the rest of the community will be very apt to suppress evidence, and to prevent the asking of questions, which would tend to yield the conclusion that this was so, and thus issue in a decision to remedy the situation. Especially when it comes to power over other people, or the distribution of material goods, people are inclined to forgo the effort of such mental activity as might lead to the conclusion that they themselves, or the immediate or wider social group to which they belong, are getting more than their due share. Members of opposed social groups, while they are liable to have blind spots of their own, will be very conscious of the deceptions thus being practised; so inter-group hatred builds up, with violence as the more or less inevitable result.

In fact it seems that, with quite depressing regularity, the truth is offensive to the pious ears of both of two opposed interest-groups, usually for opposite reasons. Anyone who asks awkward questions about his own interest-group is liable to be charged with disloyalty, with being on 'the other side', and so on; if anyone thought that the asking of such questions was always a matter of enlightened self-interest, he would know little of human nature or human affairs. Marx is surely right that such tendencies in human beings to oppress their fellows, and to rationalize the oppression with plausible self-deceptions, are exacerbated in the special circumstances of early industrial society; but I can see no reason whatever to agree with him that they will virtually disappear when technology becomes more advanced.[5]

I think that the significance of religion in general, and of Christianity in particular, for the human good, is best to be seen in its ability to counteract the mutually-reinforcing corruption of reason and will to which every human being is prone due to her individual state, and to the position in society of the groups of which she is a member. The exact meaning of the doctrine of original sin is notoriously hard to articulate;[6] but it does serve as a constant reminder of the fact that these tendencies are universal and persistent among human beings, and are not to be got rid of—for all that their effects may be ameliorated—by anything so superficial as economic or political revolution. If this is so, once the issue is squarely grasped, Christian faith and secular activity for the good of humankind may easily be seen to be most consistent and harmonious with one another.

To strip away the myths, to try to come to know the facts as they really are in defiance of individual wishful thinking and group ideology, needs a real repentance, which may amount to a crucifixion of one's former self. From this point of view one can at least understand the claim, whether one agrees with it or not, that it is in the long run only religious faith that can 'liberate human reasonableness from its ideological prisons'.[7] A sharing in the new life bestowed by God, within the communion of saints, may enable human individuals to get personal aims and group loyalties into perspective, and give them the heart to use their faculties to the best advantage for coming to know what is true and coming to do what is good. But the pressures, both internal and external, which impose conformity with the old habits are immense, and for a person clear-sightedly to set herself to overcome them would be for her to be prepared to undergo a great deal of suffering.

It is nowadays fashionable to doubt whether, now that we have some conception of the vast range of actual and potential human cultures, we can believe any longer that there is any spiritual or moral constant in humanity to which the message of Christianity could always have application.[8] But if what I have said is on the right lines, the same temptations to restrict and pervert the pursuit of truth, on behalf of oneself and one's group, will be latent in all human communities whatever, so long as there are benefits to be unfairly cornered, or chores to be inequitably evaded. The basic ingredients of the mess which is at once the basis and the consequence of human wickedness will always be the same. And it is precisely at this universal level that the Christian faith has its relevance.

If the fundamental basis for a contemporary secular ethics, and for demonstration of the relevance of religion and Christianity to this, are as obvious as I have been suggesting, it may be asked why it is not more or less universally accepted. I think that there are two principal causes, one in the recent history of theology, the other in that of philosophy. On the theological side, there has on the whole been a preoccupation with historical and exegetical studies at the expense of dogmatics; where by 'dogmatics' is meant an effort to state clearly what Christian belief amounts to, what reasons there are (if any) for believing it, and what implications it has for human living in general. If one has no clear overall grasp of what something is, it is very difficult indeed to show what point it has, if it has a point.[9] When it comes to philosophy, it appears that intellectuals in recent decades, including

17

theologians, have been scared off systematic investigation of the nature and preconditions of the human good by the fear of being bitten in the leg by moral philosophers. According to a view very widely prevalent among moral philosophers in the 1940s and 1950s, the good of human beings is not in the last resort to be determined by objective investigation, but is rather a matter of the sheer decision of the individual or the community. Fortunately, recent work in moral philosophy has tended to show that this account was an aberration.[10] It is not up to us as individuals, or even as social groups or societies, to *decide* whether or not torturing people for fun, or killing or humiliating members of human races other than our own just because they are members of such races, is wrong. A person who sincerely denied that such things were wrong would be showing rather that he was insane than that his morality, forsooth, was of an original nature yet perhaps valid in its own terms.

It is true that there is no strict logical entailment between any moral judgement and any judgement not containing moral terms; but then, as has been becoming notorious from recent studies in the philosophy of science, there is no strict logical entailment either between any series of observation-statements and any mature scientific theory, or between any mature scientific theory and any series of observational reports or experimental results not couched in terms of that theory. In fact, it appears that accounts of morality which rule out its 'objectivity' on grounds like those mentioned tend, when their principles are consistently applied, to rule out the 'objectivity' of science as well. Of course, in the case of science, for all the absence of strict entailment between theories and the results of observation, one can have excellent *grounds* in observation or experiment for saying that one theory is more likely to be true, or is a closer approximation to the truth, than another. But exactly the same applies to moral judgement; how much an action or policy tends to foster people's happiness or fulfilment, and how much it is apt to cause suffering or frustration, are relevant grounds for determining objectively whether an action or policy is really right or wrong, good or bad, as opposed to merely alleged to be so by an individual or by the majority of the members of a group.

It is often asked what is peculiar to Christian morality as such; and the response which some have recently been inclined to give, that there is nothing, has caused a good deal of distress. For the inference may seem obvious, that Christians have nothing particular to contribute to the life of society. Now I am not at all sure about the premise; I cannot make up my mind whether, and if so in what sense, Christian morality has unique and peculiar features just as such. However, I think that the inference is wrong, and that this is a matter of great importance.

Even if there were nothing peculiar to Christian morality as such, so far as particular ways of living and acting in the world are concerned, the fact that Christians have their 'life hidden with Christ in God'[11] should make, and in some cases by the grace of God actually does make, a vast difference, in giving them the heart to envisage what is true, and act for what is good, in spite of the enormous pressures of individual and group self-interest and self-deception. At her worst, the Church is just one more interest-group along with the others, jockeying for benefits and power in rivalry with them. At her best, she is the means through which there is bestowed the grace of God which is able to overcome all that self-interest and group-interest which is liable to prevent people from envisaging and striving for the general good.

Now obviously the Christian, believing as she does in the importance for one's whole destiny of a right relation with God in Christ, will have specifically religious and cultic habits in which she will express this relation, and which would be in principle pointless for unbelievers. The question is whether there are *moral* and *social* principles which are specific to Christianity as such; and I am arguing that, even if there are not, this in no way impugns the significance of the Church's role within society. Indeed, it appears to me that the discoveries of Marx, Freud and their followers about the ravages caused in the lives of individuals and of communities by self-deception enable this significance to be set out with greater clarity and force than was ever possible before. Of course, the rooting-out of self-deception in oneself is a very arduous and painful process. The point of the 'law of the Cross' which is morally so central to Christianity is that great good cannot be brought about except by self-sacrifice; this again is something which would be very obvious from the facts of the case, if only it did not suit people so well, at least in the short run, to fail to advert to it. It is so much more comfortable to suppose, against all the evidence, that outstanding moral and social problems—the plight of people in the Third World, the preserving of material resources for our grandchildren—can be solved, if only one hit on the right formula, without anguish or undue expense of effort.

Several outstanding examples of contemporary Christian witness bring home the point that I am trying to make. What is wonderful about Mother Teresa of Calcutta is not that she does good of a kind which can in principle be understood as such only by Christians; but that in the power of Christ she does what everyone can see to be good to an outstanding degree, in a way that the rest of us fail to emulate not through ignorance of the nature of the good, but because we are too fond of our pleasures and our privileges to exert ourselves so far. Archbishop Oscar Romero of El Salvador was shot at the altar not because he was saying things which were pointless or unintelligible short of reference to specifically Christian premises; but because he was discerning and denouncing as evil actions and situations which his enemies knew in their hearts to be real and to be evil, but about which they had motives for otherwise persuading themselves and others.[12]

Another case which is to the point is that of the Pro-

testant pastor who went to see the leader of an East
European People's Republic, demanding to know why
certain persons had been imprisoned. The leader, who
only understood the politics of opposed interest-groups,
said that he did not realize that the persons concerned
were members of the pastor's religious denomination.
The pastor pointed out that this was quite irrelevant; in
conniving at the imprisonments, the leader was acting
against principles of justice acknowledged by Marxists as
well as by other conscientious people.

An oppressive group or class will naturally have
stronger motive for suppressing evidence and avoiding
inconvenient questions than an oppressed; this seems to
be the truth underlying the specifically contemporary
assumption that the Church is properly the ally of left-
wing rather than right-wing political parties. But, as has
been noted by Bakunin, Orwell and others, it is one thing
for a ruling oligarchy to call itself the party which acts in
the interests of the vast majority of the people; quite
another for it actually to be so.

A number of awkward questions about the relation of
theistic religion to morality have been raised by philosophers. Does God command certain kinds of human
action to be performed, and forbid others, because such
actions are good or bad in themselves, or does the goodness and badness of human actions consist simply in the
fact that God commands and forbids them? Either possible answer has awkward consequences for the believer. If
good actions and dispositions are good only by virtue of
the fact that God commands them, then God's command,
since no reason can be given for *it*, must be arbitrary. And
the fact is that many people are able to identify some
actions as good, and others as bad, without making any
reference whatever to God's commands. However, to take
the other way out, to say that God commands and forbids
actions because they are good and bad in themselves, and
would be so whether God commanded and forbad them
or not, may well seem blasphemous to the believer. It

21

appears, at least at first sight, to imply that there is some
objective standard of moral goodness and badness, prior
to God's will and commandment, to which God's will
and commandment are morally obliged to conform. But
it is of the essence of 'God', as most people understand
the meaning of the term, that, if God exists at all, the
moral law is dependent on God's decrees, and not vice
versa.

In any case, how can we possibly *know* that what God
commands is good? It is very implausible to claim that
what one *means*, in saying that an action is good, is that it
is in accordance with God's command. In trying to find
out whether an action is good, I am likely to take various
things into account, such as the consequences, and the
motives of the agent in performing it. I need not take
God's will into account at all. Is there, then, supposed to
be a causal connection, such that God's will is supposed
somehow to bring it about that an action is good? But it
is difficult to see how the believer can have adequate
grounds for saying that such a connection exists. If she
says that she knows of the connection by faith, it may be
suspected that this apparent answer amounts to little
more than a veiled refusal to answer. And it is difficult to
make sense of the idea that she knows of the connection
through experience; she will hardly wish to say that in all
past cases, whenever we have observed God issuing a
commandment (as we frequently have done), what God
has commanded has turned out to be good.[13]

The question is discussed in Plato's dialogue *Euthyphro*.
'Piety', Euthyphro told Socrates, 'is that which is dear to
the gods, and impiety is that which is not dear to them.'[14]
But, as Socrates points out, the question then arises
'whether the pious or holy is beloved by the gods because
it is holy, or holy because it is beloved by the gods'.[15] One
is inclined to say that the holy is favoured by the gods
because it is holy; otherwise, if the favour of the gods is
not due to any quality belonging to that which they
favour, it would appear to be arbitrary. But if what is holy

is favoured by the gods on the ground that it is holy, and would be so whether they bestowed their favour upon it or not, then it follows that to be holy and to be favoured by the gods are two different things. Thus Euthyphro, in suggesting that what is holy or pious is what is favoured by the gods, can have determined at best what happens to be true of what is holy or pious; he cannot correctly have stated what it is to be holy or pious.[16]

The dilemma is no mere philosophers' quibble; it has caused a good deal of trouble at various times in the history of theology. In opposition to the main consensus of Muslim theologians, the Mu'tazilites declared that good and evil exist in the nature of things, and may be known by human reason before and apart from the direct revelation of God's will in the Koran. To this, the more orthodox objected that it was grossly presumptuous to suppose that God was bound by standards of good and evil which could be discovered by rational reflection on nature and on human affairs. God can command and forbid whatever God chooses, and what God commands and forbids are respectively good and evil; it follows that good and evil are known to humanity only through God's revelation, and not through rational reflection on a basis independent of this. Moreover, God may at any moment issue commands clean contrary to those which God has given up to now, in which case what had previously been right would be wrong.[17] Rather similar arguments, in the Christian context, were developed by William of Ockham and the Protestant Reformers against the claim that good and evil could be known independently of the revelation of God's will.

If the dilemma cannot be resolved, and the considerations which I have advanced suggest that there is at least some difficulty about resolving it, there is an obvious conclusion to be drawn. If God does exist, it is surely reasonable to hold that the divine command cannot but be the ultimate authority in moral matters. But the supposition that it is so leads apparently to intolerable contradictions. Therefore, since the supposition that there is a God leads to these contradictions, it seems reasonable to conclude that there is no God. It might plausibly be argued, along these lines, that the notion that good action is a matter of obedience to divine commands disappears insofar as a mature attitude to life is matched with a coherent philosophy; that the moral attitudes which are the consequence of theism are due to moral immaturity or philosophical incoherence or both. A theist, on this account, may be morally mature, but only at the cost of inconsistency; or she may be consistent, with the inevitable result that her moral attitudes are immature or positively repugnant. Such a view has been forcefully argued by Professor Nowell-Smith, whose account of the matter I shall summarize in the next few paragraphs.[18]

Nowell-Smith says, rightly I believe, that even if an omnipotent and omniscient Creator of the universe commands me to perform a certain action, my performance of it may still conceivably be wrong. (I cannot see any prima facie contradiction between 'A is the omnipotent and omniscient Creator of the universe' and 'A has commanded me to inflict suffering unjustly on my neighbour'—a paradigm case, one might say, of a command to do wrong. I am not sure that there is not some latent contradiction here; but I cannot show that there is, and will assume, for the purposes of the present discussion, that there is not.) He attributes to Thomas Hobbes[19] the opinion that to say that God commands by right is to say that God commands by irresistible power, and dismisses it as morally repugnant. He concludes that we must be persuaded independently of the goodness of the omnipotent Creator, even if we admit the existence of such a being, before we admit the right of such a being to command.[20]

A basic distinction is to be made, according to Nowell-Smith, between the kinds of morality in which rules are subordinated to ends, and justified as means by which these ends are to be achieved; and the kind in which the rules are absolute, in no way dependent for their validity on the good or bad consequences of obedience to them.[21] Nowell-Smith cites the psychologist Jean Piaget as having distinguished three stages in the attitude of small children towards the rules of games, of which the game of marbles may be taken as an example. At the first stage, the child just throws the marbles about in a random fashion. At the second stage, which occurs characteristically between the ages of five and nine, he regards the rules as sacred and inviolable, emanating from adults and lasting for ever. 'At this stage the child has the concept of a rule, he knows what a rule is; but he has not yet asked what a rule is *for*.' Finally, the rules are regarded as serving a purpose, the playing of a satisfactory game. Children at this final stage will not object to a modification of rules to suit special circumstances, though in the previous one they will regard this as outrageous.[22]

It is easy to see how similar the attitude of children at the second stage is to that characteristic of religious morality. 'For some Christians, the ultimate sin, the basis and . origin of all other sin, is disobedience to God. It is not the nature of murder or of perjury that makes it wrong; it is the fact that such acts are transgressions of God's commands.'[23] Similarly, good acts are not good in themselves, but only *as* acts of obedience to God. Of course, no aspersion is here being cast on *reasoned* deference to authority, for example, to one's banker in matters of finance, or to any other expert in matters within her field;[24] but this is not what the believer's submission to his God is like. Faith is *'not a reasoned trust in someone in whom we have good grounds for reposing trust;*[25] it is blind faith, utter submission of our own reason and will'. Of course, there is no denying that many theologians have tried to combine belief in God with a more enlightened moral attitude than this would suggest. But in so doing they have sacrificed consistency. (The point here is that the divine commands must either conform to what is found to be good on other grounds than that God has commanded it, or they must be wholly arbitrary. If the former is the case, there is a moral court of appeal above God; which is inconsistent with theism. So only the latter course is left.) Thus the rules attributed to the divine command *must*, in the last analysis, appear arbitrary and wholly capricious to human understanding. The theological attitude of the Protestant Reformers, which emphasized the 'total depravity' of the human being, his complete inability of himself to apprehend true goodness or to act upon it, is an illustration of this.

> *I cannot see in the subtle palliatives offered by Catholic theologians anything but evasions, vain attempts to graft a more enlightened moral outlook onto a theological tree which will not bear them. The reformers seem to me to have been right in the sense that they were restoring the original doctrine of the Church.*[26]

It would seem, then, that the belief that what is good depends upon the will of God leads to insoluble contradictions. But if God exists, then what is good must depend on God's will. Therefore the supposition that God exists leads to intolerable contradictions, and so it appears that God does not exist.

The solution to this dilemma may be summarized as follows. The question which gave rise to it is whether God's will is dependent on what is good, or what is good depends on God's will. Either of the apparently possible answers leads to awkward consequences. The real answer, I believe, is that two aspects of God's will are to be distinguished: (a) that which is supposed by believers to be communicated by special revelation, and (b) that which is to be inferred from the conditions under which creatures may individually and collectively achieve happiness and fulfilment in the world. Then (1) God's will (a) is according to what is good independently of it; (2) what is good depends on the kind of creatures women and men are and the circumstances in which they can find happiness and fulfilment; and (3) this nature of human beings and these circumstances depend on God's will (b).

For the theist, to be sure, what is good and right is ultimately dependent on the will of God, and immediately on nothing which is not ultimately determined by that will. What is apt to be overlooked by controversialists is the manner in which believers think that they come to know what the will of God is, and consequently what is good and right. According to many, and perhaps most, reflective theists, there are two principal means by which one may come by this knowledge. The first is the scrutiny of special sources alleged to contain, among other things, God's revealed will; the second is reflection on human individuals and societies in their various natural and historical situations, and on the actions and dispositions which tend in general to promote their happiness and fulfilment. (Thomas Aquinas's use of Aristotle's moral theories was based on the conviction that Aristotle was an expert on the latter aspect of things, for all that he did not have the benefit of the special revelation of God's will in Christ.) Insofar as the whole cosmic situation within which human happiness and fulfilment are to be found is dependent for its nature and existence on the will of God the creator, what is good is ultimately dependent only on that will. But so far as by 'the will of God' is meant what is revealed or alleged to be revealed in a special source of revelation, one may say that the will of God is according to what is right and good independently of it. The apparent dilemma, with all its unpalatable consequences for the theist, is due to failure to make a distinction between these two aspects of the alleged will of God; or rather, between these two means by which the one will of God is supposed to be apprehended.

Thus the believer in God may claim that she comes to know God's will both through her own experience of what tends to promote justice and happiness among her fellow human beings and through special revelation, which will differ in detail according to whether she is a

Muslim, a Zoroastrian, a Christian or a Jew. What will happen, it may be asked, if these two sources come into conflict with one another? The answer is that if a putative source of revealed divine commands radically and persistently conflicts with what is good according to the believer's own diligent inquiry into and reflection on the conditions of human happiness and justice, she ought either to cease to believe in God, or to infer that, if God has given any special revelation of God's will to human beings, it is to be found in a source other than that in which she has previously put her trust. If she continues to be a believer, and does not stop exercising her reason on moral matters, she will expect to find that such conflicts as there are between the deliverances of her own moral reasoning on the one hand, and what she can make out of God's revelation on the other, will turn out on investigation to be due either to an error in her own moral reasoning, or to misinterpretation of what has been revealed. If the honest and strenuous exercise of her intelligence and reason only reveals greater and greater discrepancies, she will have excellent grounds for abandoning her previous belief that what she took to be the source of divine revelation really was such. But, in fact, the intelligent and reasonable believer finds, or thinks that she finds, that exactly the reverse is true; that the deeper her investigation goes, the more impressive is the harmony between what is confirmed by her natural moral reasoning and what she believes God to have revealed.

It might be asked why, if God has given human beings means to reason about what is good, special revelation should be necessary at all.[27] One reason is that if, as theists characteristically believe, people are destined to enjoy or endure some form of life after death, not all of what concerns their ultimate happiness, and therefore not all the ramifications of moral good, will be scrutable to them from reflection only on this present life. In addition it may be maintained that, even so far as that aspect of good which relates merely to the present life is concerned, people are inclined, as a result either of stupidity or of self-deception, not to reason consistently or thoroughly in moral matters, and not to act in accordance with their reasoning even when they do so. One does not have to hold the Reformation doctrine of the total depravity of human beings to believe that a person's reasoning about what she ought to do is apt to be warped by prejudices deriving from her personal circumstances, her economic situation, her social class, and so on. In the believer's experience, I would have thought, the effect of the divine command is often almost exactly the opposite of that described by Nowell-Smith; it is to stimulate her moral conscience to effective action in spite of the inhibiting influence of desire and fear, and in face of the besetting tendency to self-deception in those who cannot quite forget that they ought to do what is not entirely convenient to themselves. If the atheist charges the theist with undervaluing the autonomous moral conscience of human beings, the theist may well retort that the atheist is apt to underestimate the power and persistence of the factors which interfere in its operation. To act with a view to the general good against one's own individual interests, and against the interests and prejudices of one's group, often requires heroic virtue.

On grounds of mere expedience, and quite apart from theism, one would have thought that, except in the case of those who are by nature very virtuous, there is a great difference between rules of behaviour which are such as to suit oneself, and rules of behaviour which are such as to promote the general good. Nowell-Smith writes:

> *A morality is a set of habits of choice ultimately determined by the question 'What life is most satisfactory to me as a whole?'* ... *I simply do not* understand *the suggestion that I ought to do anything that does not fit into this conception.*[28]

29

But the conception of 'what is satisfactory to me' seems to be crucially ambiguous. If it means 'what is in my own interests, whether it is in the interests of my fellow human beings or not', then I do not suppose that anyone would deny that it makes excellent sense to say 'I ought to behave in such and such a way, though the consequences of doing so will be highly unsatisfactory to myself'. But if 'what is satisfactory to me' is a matter of 'what seems morally right to me, after consideration of all the relevant issues which have occurred to me', it is doubtless true that I ought to act in a manner which is determined ultimately by the way of life which is most satisfactory to me as a whole. But the two senses of the phrase 'what is satisfactory to me' are very different from one another. To take this difference seriously is a central characteristic of theism, and not only in its Christian form. A person sees what she ought to do, which is very far from being 'satisfactory to herself' in the normal sense of the expression; she fails miserably in her attempts to do it; and so comes to submit herself to a power which she thinks there is good reason to suppose will ultimately enable her to do what she knows she ought to do.[29] To believe in God is to believe in a universal context in which people will not ultimately get away either with the moral renunciation of refusing to try to pursue the good, or with the self-deception which consists of declining to advert to it. They may be *forgiven*; but that is quite another matter.

It might further be asked whether the two aspects of the divine will which I have distinguished might not conceivably contradict one another. Could an omnipotent and omniscient creator of the world not issue commands which, according to criteria derived from intelligent reflection on the flourishing of human individuals and societies, were bad? But even supposing that this is possible, my argument here is not affected; all that is essential to it is that it is *self-consistent* to suppose, as theists do, that the omnipotent and omniscient creator in fact issues commands which are good. Indeed, if the commands issued by an omnipotent and omniscient creator were bad on all other counts than the mere fact that such a being had issued them, it would be very misleading to call that being 'God' without qualification.

It appears, then, that what is good and right in human actions and dispositions depends ultimately on the divine will, if God exists; since in that case the whole context of human life within which moral terms have their application, and from which they derive their significance, depends on it. Any alleged source of God's special revealed will commends itself as such by being fundamentally harmonious with the thorough application of intelligence and reason to the problems of individual and social life. As Nowell-Smith sees it, if God is to be God, God's will and commandment must in the last resort be wholly arbitrary. I would have thought, on the contrary, that if God is to be God, God's will and commandment must be supremely reasonable. This appears to be only one illustration among many of the remarkable differences between the God in whom many theists believe, and the God in whom many atheists disbelieve.

What, then, is the relation between morality and belief in God? It is *not* the case that no human being of good will can fail to believe in God, or be the adherent of some religion. It is *not* the case that no human being of good will can justify or articulate her moral stance without appeal to religious belief. It has been important for my argument, indeed, that one can have a perfectly clear and correct conception of what kinds of people and actions are morally good, and what kinds morally bad, without any kind of appeal to God or religion. The significance of religion for morality relates not so much to the *definition* of the good, one might put it, as to its *implementation*. In the present scheme of things, the innocent, and those who exert themselves in the cause of general happiness and justice, are subjected to misery and degradation not only *in spite of*, but quite often *because of*, their moral goodness. (That is to say that their respect for the good leads them

31

to perform actions for which they are persecuted; not that their persecutors actually put it to themselves that they are persecuting them *because* they—the persecuted—are acting virtuously.) Short of belief in God, or some other belief which is equivalent in the relevant respect,[30] there is no good reason to believe that happiness is at all proportionate to desert; and there are indeed excellent prudential grounds at once for being rather bad, and for pretending that one is better than one is.[31] Now the eschatological doctrines of the great religions are notoriously various; but they do seem to have in common that they entail the following: that happiness is ultimately roughly in proportion to desert, that the bullies and cheats who flourish in this world will not ultimately benefit from acting as they do. The falsity of this proposition is not a possibility that the person of good will, if she sees the matter clearly, can contemplate with any complacency. She must *want* it to be true that in the long run oppressors will not derive advantage from their oppression, that the innocent and upright will ultimately achieve fulfilment at least approximately in accordance with their virtue. I conclude that the clear-sighted person of good will must wish that theism, or at least something with equivalent eschatological implications, were true; or at any rate that she cannot regard its falsity as less than a moral tragedy. Perhaps it is worth reminding the reader that what is immediately at issue is not whether theism is true; but whether, if true, it would be relevant to morality.

Notes

1 The widespread interest in techniques of meditation is one sign of this.
2 I owe this citation to Professor Philip Thody.
3 E. Heimler, *Mental Illness and Social Work* (Harmondsworth, 1967).

4 An invaluable summary of accounts of the great sociologists on the effects of social change, and the relevance of religion to them, is to be had in Gregory Baum's *Religion and Alienation* (New York, 1975).

5 Cf. D. McLellan, *The Thought of Karl Marx: An Introduction* (London, 1971), p. 109.

6 For a useful survey and discussion of contemporary accounts, see G. Vandervelde, *Original Sin* (Amsterdam, 1975).

7 B. Lonergan, *Method in Theology* (London, 1971), p. 117.

8 Thus Dennis Nineham will have it that 'to posit "an unchangeable fundamental structure of the human spirit as such" ' is 'a very doubtful thing to do': *The Myth of God Incarnate*, ed. John Hick (London, 1977), p. 200.

9 On the splintered and fragmentary state of contemporary theological studies, cf. Karl Rahner, *Foundations of Christian Faith* (London, 1978), p. 6. Though as Alan Sell has remarked, 'there is almost too much "popular" dogmatics which is either conservatively pre-critical, or liberally ahistorical'.

10 'Emotivism' in ethics is well represented by C. L. Stevenson, *Ethics and Language* (New Haven, 1944), while the classic of 'prescriptivism' is R. M. Hare, *The Language of Morals* (Oxford, 1952). For the reaction against such accounts in more recent philosophy, see Anthony Quinton, *The Nature of Things* (London, 1973), chapter 12; Bernard Williams, *Morality* (Cambridge, 1972), pp. 57–61; and Alasdair MacIntyre, *After Virtue* (Notre Dame, 1981).

11 Colossians 3:3.

12 For a brief description of the sort of thing that Archbishop Romero was saying, see *The Times* (31 March 1980).

13 The substance of this paragraph is derived from W. W. Bartley, *Morality and Religion* (London and Basingstoke, 1971), pp. 8–9.

14 Plato, *Euthyphro*, 6e–7a. I quote from Jowett's translation.

15 Ibid., 9e.

16 Ibid., 10e–11b.

17 Cf. H. A. R. Gibb, 'Islam' in *The Concise Encyclopaedia of Living Faiths*, ed. R. C. Zaehner (London, 1959), p. 199.

18 P. H. Nowell-Smith, 'Morality, religious and secular' in

Christian Ethics and Contemporary Philosophy, ed. I. T. Ramsey (London, 1966), pp. 95–112.

19 Cf. *Leviathan*, chapter 31. In fact, as Professor P. T. Geach has pointed out to me, it is not clear that this is precisely Hobbes's position.

20 Nowell-Smith, op. cit., p. 97.

21 Ibid., p. 98.

22 Ibid., pp. 101–2.

23 Ibid., pp. 103–4.

24 Ibid., p. 97.

25 My italics.

26 Nowell-Smith, op. cit., pp. 104, 106.

27 The whole of this argument owes a great deal to Thomas Aquinas; and this is specially true of the matter in this paragraph. Cf. *Summa Theologica* I, i, 1; *Summa Contra Gentiles* I, 4.

28 Nowell-Smith, op. cit., p. 108.

29 This comes out with special clarity, I think, in the work of Martin Luther.

30 Whatever differences there are between the doctrines of reincarnation and *karma* in the Eastern religions on the one hand, and the belief in heaven and hell in the Western religions on the other, they have much the same relevance to morality.

31 The point is admirably made by Glaucon and Adeimantus at the beginning of the second book of Plato's *Republic*.

T W O

On Christianity and the religions

'But even if there were a God, and even if belief in God were positively useful for morality, how could one reasonably assent to the special claims of Christianity in face of the conflicting doctrines of other religions?'

Very roughly, religions are characterized by:
  (a) liturgical habits
  (b) moral ideals and conceptions of salvation
  (c) stories
  (d) beliefs about what is, has been or will be the case.

Anthropologists, I believe, sometimes speculate whether myth or ritual, 'word' or 'sacrament', came first in the evolution of religion in general or of particular religions. At least, in fully developed religions, there is generally a set of liturgical procedures (a) which is justified by reference to a story or set of stories (c); in enactment of the one and meditation on the other a new and better form of life (b) is held to be afforded in the present or assured for the future or both. In the eucharist, for example, Christians say that they share the sacrifice of Christ which took place once and for all at Golgotha. In this symbolical sharing in the sacrifice of Christ that is both described and reflected upon in the documents of the New Testament, they understand themselves to be partaking of a new and better form of life ('life in Christ') which is gradually supplanting the old and corrupt way of living. Much the same applies, *mutatis mutandis*, to other kinds of religion.

So far as aspects (a), (b) and (c) of religion are concerned, divergences between the religions are only remotely analogous to disagreements about matters of fact. Cultured Hindus will say that each person should follow her own *dharma*—that is to say, should meditate on the stories, cultivate the moral ideal, and engage in the rituals, which correspond to her own cultural milieu and personal needs. Of course the issues in the case of religion, even as restricted to these aspects, are still momentous; whether an individual can get through life without resorting to crime or insanity may depend on whether or not she gets involved in a religion, and which religion she gets involved in. But disagreements between adherents of different religions, or between adherents of religion and those of no religion, are not, when these aspects of the matter only are taken into account, such that for one party to be believing truly is for the other party to be believing falsely.

What makes the crucial difference is aspect (d) of religious belief—belief about what is the case. Now most traditional Christians, as well as those of other faiths, have believed that the truth of their religious belief entailed that certain states of affairs had been, were, or would be the case; and that if these states of affairs were not the case, their belief would be false. Those who think that this factual element in Christianity is only peripheral to it[1] have to remember that the apostle Paul clearly states that, if there be no resurrection from the dead, Christian faith is vain; and that there is no reason to believe that there will be such a future resurrection, unless Christ is truly risen from the dead.[2]

In a very limited sense, I believe, every religious person as such is involved in *some* belief in particular matters of fact. A person might perhaps fail to believe in any form of afterlife, and deny any but a minimal historical content in the gospels, and yet feel the compelling power of the gospel story, enabling her to become a better person, and to achieve serenity or patience in face of the insignificance or the anguish of her life. But at any rate *that* meditation on the gospel story, with or without public worship or liturgical activity, has this effect upon her, is a matter of contingent fact that *happens* to be so when it *might* not have been so. Yet there is a difference of a profound kind between a person whose belief is characterized by assent only to this kind of matter of fact, and one who sets store by the historical or eschatological tenets of the great religions.

Someone who called herself a Christian, a Hindu, or a Mahayana Buddhist might argue rather like this: 'I neither know nor care whether there is any historical validity whatever in any of the traditional documents of my faith; or whether there is any form of life after death available to any person, either in the form of reincarnation, or of resurrection, or of the survival of a disembodied soul. But what I do know, beyond all shadow of doubt, is the saving power of my religion here and now, as I meditate upon its stories and take part in its liturgy. You may ask what I mean by this "saving power". The answer is, its capacity to enhance tremendously my life here and now, giving it an inner harmony and peace far beyond what material enjoyments, or even the more sophisticated enjoyments afforded by the arts, can provide; and furthermore, to enable me to lead a life that is morally better and more contributory to the good of those among whom I live than would otherwise be possible.'

This aspect of religious belief, as immediately self-authenticating, and so not subject to validation by any state of affairs beyond what can be known immediately by the believer, has been well expressed by C. G. Jung. As Jung sees it, a psychotherapist can often help a patient by encouraging her to take to some form of religion. He remarks that a rationalist might well accuse the therapist in such a case of 'replacing an honest neurosis with the swindle of religious belief'. But he points out that it will be an instance not so much of *belief* in the ordinary sense as of *experience*—of the healing and transforming power of religious symbols, rituals and stories. As to the question of 'belief' in the more restricted sense, 'no one can know what the ultimate things are. We must therefore take them as we experience them. And if such experience helps to make life healthier, more beautiful, more satisfactory to yourself and to those you love, you may safely say: "This was the grace of God".'[3] The ultimate truth in these matters, he is saying, must be forever withheld from us. Meanwhile, the religions give many people a measure of insight into, control over, and happiness in their lives, which, it seems, can be obtained for them by no other means. And is this not as much proof as there could possibly be that there is 'truth' of a kind, and of however unscientific a kind, in them?

This is all very well, so long as the question of 'truth' in religion is deemed to be exclusively a matter of its authentication in the adherent's life here and now, and not a matter of states of affairs (like the existence of a historical figure who said and did roughly what the four gospels say he said and did, and the possibility of life after death in at least some form for at least some persons) which have no intrinsic relation to what is a matter of immediate experience here and now. It is characteristic of religions that they include some kind of doctrine of the future life. Even Theravada Buddhism, the religion which can perhaps claim with some justice to be the most stringently empirical, and is agnostic about the existence of God and denies the substantiality of the human soul, can be said to be dependent on some form at least of the doctrine of reincarnation. Why submit to the austerities of the Noble Eightfold Path, after all, if blessed annihilation will be ours in any case after a long life of pleasure? The doctrine fundamental to Buddhism, that all pleasure has to be paid for in the long run by an excess of frustration and suffering, is not, to say the least of it, something that can be established by reflection on human experience as we know it within the bounds of a single life span. There are many human lives which, unless reincarnation be assumed, are as strong evidence against the doctrine as can possibly be imagined. Other schools of Buddhism, and the various sects of Hinduism, are just as clearly committed to belief in an afterlife. Christianity is in an even more embarrassing situation than Hinduism or Buddhism in this respect, since it is clearly committed, at least in anything like its traditional form, to certain specific and at first sight very improbable judgements of historical fact. A sophisticated Hindu, if she were asked whether Krishna in fact appeared to Arjuna in the form of the latter's charioteer (as alleged in the *Bhagavad Gita*), might well dismiss the question as quite insignificant for her religion; but a Christian cannot really admit the gospels to be entirely or almost entirely mythical or legendary, without denying her faith in any but a very etiolated form. As to element (d) of religion, then, I conclude that most religions have some kind of eschatological commitment, and that some religions—especially Christianity, and perhaps to a lesser extent Judaism and Islam—have a historical commitment as well.

Evidently 'salvation' will have a different meaning for a religious person according to whether or not she takes seriously the eschatological commitment of her religion. If she does not, her present conviction of 'rightness with God' or conformity with the universal order of things, her present conquest of sin and serenity in the face of pain and anxiety, will provide the full context of what salvation means for her. But if she does take the eschatological commitment of her religion into account, such present experience will at best be a *sign* of the full and total salvation which she awaits in the future. (Thus Paul calls the present life of Christians in the Spirit a pledge of what is yet to come.[4]) Contrariwise, the present conviction of well-being of those who defy God, who do not live in accordance with *Tao*, who have bad *karma*, is in a sense no mistake; it is so only if taken as an index of what their ultimate fate will be. I do not think the Theravada Buddhist would be inclined to deny that the delight of many people in sensual indulgence is real enough so far as it goes; the only catch is that, whatever may immediately appear, it will also have to be paid for later, in suffering or frustration.

Given the account which I have suggested of what it is to be the adherent of a religion, some answer may be attempted to the question of whether, and if so to what extent, the adherent of one religion could claim that her own religion was uniquely true. There are two extreme views to be taken into account on this: (a) that there is nothing whatever in common between the beliefs of one religion and another, or (more usually) at least those of one's own religion and those of others; and (b) that every religion expresses what is essentially the same thing in different ways. To the first thesis, the obvious objection can be raised that several religions—Christianity, Islam, Judaism, and at least one form of Hinduism—involve belief in a God who is the unique cause of all else that exists, and who is conceived closely on the analogy of a person, in such a way that one may talk with God, be more or less devoted to God, and obey or disobey God's commands. A follower of Karl Barth would say that the meaning of everything that the Christian says about God is determined, or at least *ought* to be determined, by the fact that the God in question is none other than the God revealed in Jesus Christ.[5] Thus all the divine attributes— omnipotence, omniscience, creativity, and so on—are to be understood in the light of Jesus Christ; and it is held to follow that the alleged 'Gods' of other religions, even though they are called omnipotent, omniscient, infinitely good, and so on, can have nothing to do with the true God. Karl Barth was, of course, a Christian theologian; but it does not require any very strenuous exercise of the imagination to see how the adherent of any other system of religious belief could take exactly the same line. Now I would agree that, for the Christian, her whole conception of God is fundamentally coloured by what she believes to be God's culminating self-revelation in Jesus Christ; but, just the same, it seems to me that, so far as words can be trusted at all, many non-Christian conceptions of God come very close to the Christian conception. And it would seem to be a more or less insuperable objection to this view, that Jews and Muslims believe along with Christians that the Old Testament is in some sense a record of the revelation of God. Does it not seem absurd for a Christian to deny that these people have some conception of the God whom the Christian claims to be revealed in a unique manner in Jesus Christ, when so many of the statements which are made about 'God' by the non-Christians concerned, and so many of their attitudes to God, are demonstrably similar to the statements and attitudes of Christians?

The opposite view, that all religions convey fundamentally the same teaching, also seems to me more or less demonstrably wrong, and for a very similar reason. If the prima facie meanings of words are to be trusted at all, there is little if anything that all the principal religions of the world teach in common. F. Heiler sees belief in a personal God and desire for loving communion with this God as a fundamental characteristic of religion.[6] This, at least, is a thesis which seems at first sight obviously incorrect, except on a very restricted definition of 'religion' which does not conform to ordinary usage. Theravada Buddhism and Jainism are on the most obvious interpretation atheistic, and are at the very least compatible with atheism; and the Advaita school of Hinduism, with its absolute monism, is theistic at most in a peculiar or extended sense. More promising, it seems to me, is A. N. Whitehead's suggestion that what the universal religious consciousness of humankind is witness to is the thesis that there is an objective norm to which one has an intuition of more or less corresponding or failing to correspond.[7] This is close to William James's characterization of the teaching common to all religions; the existence of something wrong with us, and the availability of a means of putting this wrongness right.[8] One is 'saved', now or hereafter or both, as a result of correspondence with this norm or application of this means; failure to correspond with or apply which tends to lead to frustration and despair in the individual and bewilderment and disruption in society. Only in theistic religions is this norm seen in terms of the will of a personal God.

However inadequate Heiler's account as applied to religion as such, it does seem to provide a useful characterization of theism. One might conceive Whitehead's and Heiler's accounts on the analogy of the outer and inner rings of a target of which Christianity is at the centre. No value-judgement is thereby immediately implied. It might well be argued that to be bound by the more universal testimony of the human religious consciousness is the more rational course; and one would be constrained thereby to remain in the outer ring. Dogmatic Christianity would then be rather a gross and extravagant example of what William James termed an 'overbelief'.

Let us say that a religious story which expresses and satisfies human aspiration in the kind of way that I have tried to describe is 'profoundly true'. In that case we may distinguish four types of religious disagreement:

(1) Disagreement about what is literally true.
(2) Disagreement about what is 'profoundly true'.
(3) Conceptual disagreement.
(4) Practical disagreement.

Religious disagreement may, certainly, be about a matter of fact in a quite ordinary sense—as was noticed by those who described the apostle Paul's dispute with his Jewish opponents as one about whether a particular historical individual called Jesus was dead or not.[9] Among

42

factual disagreements would be disagreement about whether there is any form of afterlife in any circumstances for human beings, and what bearing people's present belief and practice had on their fate in this life or the next. Or disagreement may be about a matter of what is 'profoundly true'—whether any religious story and attendant set of practices whatever, or whether some particular one, is ultimately satisfying or worthwhile (in the kind of way I tried to describe by reference to Jung) to a particular person or to persons of a particular society, or to humankind at large. I will discuss these two types of disagreement at greater length below; first it will be useful to get the other two types of disagreement out of the way.

Arguments between people who can usefully be described as of the same religion will commonly be primarily of a conceptual or practical kind. Thus Arius and Athanasius in the fourth century, Socinians and Trinitarians in the sixteenth, did not disagree on such matters as whether the historical Jesus was as the gospels describe him, or on the general outlines of eschatology. They disagreed on the question of whether Jesus Christ should be held to be really and truly God or not—one might say, not on the *facts* of the case, but their *interpretation*. (Of course, this kind of disagreement does not stand on its own, as the enemies of dogmatic theology are inclined to suppose; it has ramifications of factual and practical kinds. One may compare the case of theoretical physics where two authorities might agree about a particular range of experimental results, but disagree profoundly about their theoretical implications; and no one would doubt that theoretical physics has in the long run plenty of factual and practical consequences.) Practical disagreement in religion may be of a moral or a liturgical kind—whether you go to war or not in a particular situation, whether you receive communion in both kinds or not. This type of disagreement, though of course of great practical importance, does not offer the same problems of understanding as the others, and so can be passed over very briefly in the present context.

As to claims about 'profound truth', it is clear that the Christian story has a great deal in common with the stories which characterize other religions. 'One day she conceived the fruit of her womb, but without any defilement.' If that excerpt from the Buddhist scripture *The Legend of Shakyamuni* has nothing to do with the Christian doctrine of the Virgin Birth, and still more with the specifically Roman Catholic doctrine of the Immaculate Conception,[10] I do not know what it would be for any doctrine or story in one religion to have anything to do with any doctrine or story in another. Odin and Attis hung on trees, as Jesus hung on a cross; there were already crosses and victims on them in primitive America, when the Christian missionaries first arrived there. The Aztecs ate their maize god; the primitive Persians drank theirs in the form of an intoxicating liquor; Christians, inveterately syncretist in this matter as in every other, eat and drink their God. As Joel Carmichael has written:

> It has been obvious for years that Christianity contains at the very least 'a morsel of paganism'. A mere resume of Pauline Christianity—which gave the Church its definitive shape, after all—indicates this: A Divine Being, the Son of the Lord of the Universe, is miraculously born on earth to play his role in the struggle between Good and Evil. As part of the Divine Plan, the Being is painfully put to death; the individual worshipper, identifying himself with this being via the Redemptive Crucifixion, is guaranteed personal salvation. This is plainly the same structure as in many pagan mysteries of the Old Near East; it has been streamlined, universalised and above all dramatised by being hinged to the fate of an historic individual. Paul himself made no bones about calling it a 'mystery'; when the doctors of the early Church fought the 'false' mysteries they knew what they were doing.[11]

Now traditional Christianity, as in some sense the 'fulfilment' of other religions (rather than utterly different in kind from them or merely one among them, as on the extreme views I have already mentioned), commends itself precisely as the meeting through a *historical* narrative of needs and aspirations expressed in myths, and apparently not only the myths of the ancient Near East, but those of the whole world. On this view of the matter, the question whether there *was* a real historical fulfilment, or whether a particular bit of history of an initially less exotic shape was subsequently supplied by the folk imagination with mythological garnishings, becomes of crucial importance. To be true in anything like the sense Christians have traditionally supposed that it is, in other words, Christianity must not only be 'profoundly true' in the way that all the other great religions at least to some extent demonstrably are; it must also be, and I think must be more or less unique in being, literally true into the bargain. And since the literal truth of Christianity implies the literal truth of a number of rather curious historical assertions, about a man's birth from a virgin, his performance of miracles, and his resurrection from the dead, Christianity will be vulnerable to the criticisms of historians to a degree that other religions, which do not set store so essentially by historical beliefs as such, are not. The criterion of Christian truth cannot be only 'Does meditation on and ritual participation in this collection of stories and doctrines do for you what other religions do for you, and more?'—but also 'Did the events narrated by the stories, or at least something very like them, really happen?'

The 'profound truth' of religions, that in them which meets human need and aspiration, can take one or more of at least three forms. R. C. Zaehner and others have distinguished between 'prophetic' and 'mystical' religion.[12] Mystical religion is preoccupied with the discovery of eternity within you, and is not communicable except by way of long association between master and disciple; it is little concerned with the external affairs of the world. Prophetic religion typically involves an alleged direct communication from a personal transcendent God, through a prophet, to a community or to all humankind, with immediate and pressing significance for life in this world. In general, mystical religion stresses individual salvation, prophetic religion salvation in and through a community. On the whole one can say that Hinduism represents the mystical type of religion, Islam the prophetic; while Christianity is essentially a kind of fusion between the two. It is of some interest that, as Zaehner shows, religions of each type tend, in the course of their history, to develop features characteristic of the other—as though the need met by the other kind had also to express itself. Thus the Sufi movement in Islam is decidedly mystical in tendency, while the *Bhagavad-Gita*, with its stress on communication from a personal transcendent God, represents a complementary trend in Hinduism.

But there is a third essential element in Christianity which is not readily reducible to the 'prophetic' or the 'mystical', and which seems to be characteristic rather of what are sometimes called 'lower' religions. Typical of this 'lower' element in Christianity are (1) the prominence of a 'cult-hero', a divine or semi-divine protagonist in a cosmic drama; and (2) the centrality of the group of ideas associated with the Eucharist, which involves participation in the life of the god by way of a sacrificial meal. Where the matter of cult-heroes is concerned, it seems, once again, that there is a tendency in great religions which are not intrinsically based upon such an idea to make a compromise with it. The Buddha whose significance at first is only that he has achieved enlightenment and proclaims the *dharma*, becomes the Lord Buddha, himself an object of worship, in the Mahayana tradition; and Muhammad suffers a not dissimilar fate at the hands of some Sufis. As Zaehner comments of incarnation, 'This seems to be another, though less general "truth" that is liable to turn up in all religions'; and he adds immediately the important comment, 'but *only* in Christianity is it crucial'.[13]

Zaehner did well, in my opinion, to put the word 'truth' in inverted commas in the last quotation. He defines truth at one point as 'that which corresponds to the deepest instincts of mankind'; which amounts to what I called 'profound truth'. We are now in some position, I think, to make sense of the view that Christianity is the uniquely true religion, whether we agree with it or not. Such a claim makes sense if taken to imply (a) that there are in Christianity, so to speak written into its constitution and not added as a result of subsequent developments, elements satisfying the points of view expressed in prophetic, mystical and 'lower' religions; (b) that its 'story' is on the whole a matter of historical fact, though containing elements, the miracles, of great prima facie improbability; (c) that these two features are together characteristic only of Christianity among the world-religions. 'Pagans are wrong and Christians are right' says the *Chanson de Roland*; but if the account I have suggested is at all on the right lines, it will follow, on the contrary, that if Christianity were true, the other religions would each have at least some part of the truth.

The account which I have just given of the relation of Christianity to other religions differs a good deal from some others which have recently been put forward. As John Hick sees it, all the religions testify, from their different points of view, to the existence and nature of God; where there is apparent doctrinal conflict, at least in important matters, this is due to the differing cultural backgrounds of those who propound the doctrines. For example, if a Muslim says that God's nature and will are uniquely revealed in the Koran, she is really, or should really be, expressing the fact that the Koran has this status for her and for other Muslims, but is not, or should not be, denying that other books, persons or institutions have or ought to have the same status and function for Christians, Hindus, or Buddhists.[14] Hick compares the traditional Christian view, which *mutatis mutandis* may be found in other religions as well, according to which one's own religious belief is as it were at the centre of the religious universe, with the Ptolemaic conception of the motion of the sun and planets round the stationary earth on which one happened to live oneself. According to his own 'Copernican' view, it is *God*, and not *Christ*, who is at the centre of the 'universe of faiths', all of which have their own equally valid perspective on the divine mystery.

This view of the matter has obvious attractions, especially at a time when Christians, provided they are not dinosaurs or Barthians, are acutely conscious of the treasures of knowledge and wisdom enshrined in religious traditions other than their own, and of their own lamentable failure in the past to recognize them. But I do not see how it can really resolve any fundamental problem. Its ecumenical advantages are more apparent than real.[15] If belief in God tends to unite Christians with Jews and Muslims and many Hindus, it leaves them as far divided as ever from Theravada Buddhists, Marxists and secular humanists. And relegation of belief in an incarnate God to a mere *façon de parler* would seem to be a loss of possible points of contact between traditional Christianity on the one hand, and Mahayana Buddhism, Vaishnavite Hinduism, and much primitive religion on the other. Vishnu in India has many incarnations, which have a vital role in popular piety, for all that they have very little historical corroboration.[16] A common phenomenon in primitive religion is belief in what is termed a *deus otiosus*, who originally created the cosmos and propounded the moral law, but who now takes little notice of either; together with much more palpable involvement with the career of a divine-human demigod or hero.[17] As to the Mahayana, it is said to be characteristic of one of its schools to believe that

> *the Buddha was transcendent, supramundane, eternal and infinite. The historical Buddha was only a fictitious*

*person sent by Him to appear in the world, to assume a
human body, to live like an ordinary human being and
teach the* dharma *to the inhabitants of the world. The
real Buddha is the reality* par excellence.[18]

The analogy in each of these cases with the Christian
account of Christ is striking.[19]

From the viewpoint of Wilfred Cantwell Smith, if we
reject the view that each religion is a single entity, and
realize the doctrinal, institutional and cultic variety within
each 'religion', and the close connection between each of
its constitutive elements and those of other 'religions',
then apparent doctrinal disagreements between
'religions' will disappear, or at least become easier to
handle.[20] However, this approach seems to me not so
much to clear up the problem of differing beliefs about
what is so between the great religions, as to brush it under
the carpet. What is the evidence that the problem will
really become any more amenable when we cease to distinguish between Christianity and Islam, say, as each a
different 'religion', attending to the variety within each
'religion', and to the features it shares with or has taken
over from other 'religions'? If any supposed cognitive
content of 'Christianity' or 'Islam' is as contentious
between Christians and Christians, or between Muslims
and Muslims, as it is between Christians and Muslims, is
not the problem of cognitive disagreement between
religious persons worsened rather than ameliorated? The
fact is that every attempt to tackle the problem of conflicting faiths or ideologies has to take into account the truth,
as inconvenient as it is unavoidable, that *so long as your
faith or ideology has any cognitive content at all, or any factual
implications which are not trivial, some persons of intelligence
and good will are going to disagree with you.* This problem
cannot be spirited away by pretending that cognitive content is not essential to faith, or by making it implausibly
vague.

Notes

1 D. Z. Phillips is perhaps the most eloquent exponent of this point of view. See *The Concept of Prayer* (London, 1967).

2 1 Corinthians 15:12–14.

3 C. G. Jung, *Psychology and Religion* (*Collected Works*, vol. XI; London, 1958), p. 104.

4 Ephesians 1:13–14.

5 This point is made over and over again in Barth's *Church Dogmatics* (Edinburgh, 1936–64), perhaps especially in Volume I.

6 F. Heiler, 'The history of religions as a preparation for the cooperation of religions' in *The History of Religions*, ed. M. Eliade and J. Kitagawa (Chicago, 1959).

7 A. N. Whitehead, *Religion in the Making* (Cambridge, 1926), p. 66.

8 William James, *The Varieties of Religious Experience* (London, 1910), p. 508.

9 Acts 25:19.

10 I understand that most authorities would deny that the virgin birth of the Buddha is being suggested here; it is rather his immaculate conception.

11 Joel Carmichael, review of J. M. Allegro, *The Sacred Mushroom and the Cross*, *Observer* (17 May 1970).

12 Zaehner presents his position briefly in a paper 'Religious truth', which I have only seen in typescript. The distinction between 'prophetic' and 'mystical' religion has, of course, become widely accepted.

13 Zaehner, ibid.

14 See J. Hick, *God and the Universe of Faiths* (London and Basingstoke, 1973).

15 Cf. J. Hick, 'Jesus and the world religions' in *The Myth of God Incarnate*, ed. Hick (London, 1973), pp. 167–85.

16 See R. C. Zaehner, *Concordant Discord* (Oxford, 1970), p. 443.

17 See M. Eliade, *Patterns of Comparative Religion* (London, 1958).

18 Jaidev Singh, *An Introduction to Madhyamaka Philosophy* (Delhi, 1976), p. 7.
19 The last quotation, of course, is parallel to a Docetic rather than an orthodox Christology.
20 Cf. especially Wilfred Cantwell Smith, *The Meaning and End of Religion* (New York, 1964) and *Towards a World Theology* (Philadelphia, 1981).

THREE

Incarnation and atonement

'Let us admit for a moment that the differences between the religions can be accounted for by the Christian in the kind of way you describe. The doctrines of the incarnation and the atonement still ought to prevent any reasonable person from believing in Christianity. Recently, many theologians have themselves been driven to the admission that the doctrine of the incarnation is erroneous, or confused, or out-of-date, or a mythical expression of some truth which might better be expressed in another way, or something else of the sort. The doctrine of the atonement is immoral as well as irrational, implying as it does the monstrous proposition that one person can justly be punished for crimes committed by others.'

Certainly, it is central to Christian belief *that* God has wrought the salvation of humankind in Jesus Christ, and that this includes counteracting the effects of sin. The question of *how* God has done so, and in what manner we are to understand the act of God in Christ on our behalf, has always exercised theologians. The explanation that God has set us a good example in the life of Christ has not usually commended itself as adequate to believers; on the other hand, the notion that Jesus Christ has paid to the devil (Augustine) or to the Father (Anselm) a price that we could not have paid for ourselves has been stigmatized as artificial. That Christ is to be thought of as victor over the powers of evil (Aulén) does not seem so much to be an explanation as another way of putting what has to be explained. Substitutionary theories of the atonement, where Christ suffers in the place of other human beings what their sins deserve, are often and not implausibly said to presuppose an odd idea of God and an odder idea of morality.

Now, the doctrine of the incarnation is presented, as one finds in effect in many places in Scripture and the traditional documents of the churches, as a divine response to a human problem, the human problem being that of sin and its effects. How, one may ask, is the solution which is the incarnation supposed to meet the problem of sin? Can we, as it were, get any insight into the biochemistry of the process through which the divine medicine is alleged to cure the human disease?

Many theists, for example Jews and Muslims, have always claimed that the doctrine of the incarnation was false. Recently, the view has been gaining ground that it is 'true for' certain people, in the sense that it is their way of expressing what could be put more precisely and coherently in a different way.[1] I think it is important to say something about what it might be for a belief to be 'true for' one person or group, 'false for' another person or group, before we go any further. Ordinary people, without scholarly sophistication, are apt to be irritated by the suggestion that belief in God or in Christ might be 'true for' George or the people of Dallas, 'false for' Leonid or the people of Leningrad; and in my opinion they have considerable grounds for such irritation. God, they feel, is like Table Mountain or the Sea of Azov in that God's existence is not dependent on the say-so of any individual or community; and consequently, if God does exist, those who deny that God exists are just wrong, and if God does not exist, they are right. What is directly at issue here, however, is strictly speaking not a *theological* but a *Christological* relativism. The kind of thinker that I have in mind would concede that *God* is not such that God's existence depends on the attitude that any particular person or group may happen to take to God; they would deny that God is like J. M. Barrie's Tinker Bell, who was dependent for her existence on people's belief in her. But they would argue that the unique presence of God in Jesus Christ is a matter of how the followers of Jesus have responded to him, what they have 'found in' him, rather than of what is actually the case about Jesus, and would have been so whether his followers had thus reacted to him or not.

Let us call the thesis that the incarnation is in the last analysis a matter of the reaction of Jesus' followers to him the 'soft view' of the incarnation; and the thesis that it is a matter of what actually is the case about Jesus himself, whatever the attitude of his followers, the 'hard view'. I should say immediately that it is the 'hard view' with which I shall primarily be concerned, not the 'soft'. On the 'soft view', the doctrine of the incarnation is in any case trivially true—no one doubts that many people have 'seen God in Jesus', that in the stories, true or false, which have come down to us about Jesus, they have been brought in a unique degree to what they call 'the presence of God', and have felt that they have learned how it is between humanity and God, and so on. The question I shall be concerned with is whether there might be any reason to believe in the incarnation *tout court*, not whether the doctrine has expressed an attitude which has been widely held and still might be worth holding.

It is not that such a way of talking would necessarily be unsuitable when applied to every analogous case. Suppose that an ancient Babylonian describes the retreat of the Euphrates floods as the victory of Marduk over Tiamat. In this case I think one can properly say of the Babylonian that it is 'true for him' that when the floods first show signs of receding, Marduk is beginning his victory over Tiamat. While a more comprehensive and sophisticated view of reality would put his way of talking out of court, one can still make sense of it and recognize a certain conditional validity in it. Similarly, it seems to me, one might say of an unreconstructed Christian, 'The incarnation is true for her', if a more comprehensive account than hers of God, humankind, and the role of Jesus between God and humankind, brought out that the doctrine of the incarnation as interpreted on the 'hard view' was false. One way of approaching the question before us is to inquire whether, as a result of modern investigations into history or philosophy or comparative religion or what have you, the incarnation ought to be conceded to have at best this relative sort of validity, and to be false as interpreted according to the 'hard view'.

So much for some clearing of the ground. Does the alleged divine solution of the incarnation, as understood on the 'hard view', appear to meet the problem of human sin and its consequences? Since sin is a disorder in human behaviour, it appears to me that one should look for evidence bearing on this question in fields of inquiry which bear on human individual and group behaviour. Now the roots of moral evil in human beings are many and hotly disputed; but I think that it would be almost universally agreed that a large part of the moral evil that exists is due to the human tendency to mutual combativeness, which may culminate in anything from a scuffle between children or a mild display of academic waspishness to the horrors of genocide or total war. Anyone who is at all seriously concerned with the fate of the human race must occasionally ask herself what circumstances tend to the evocation or control of this besetting human tendency to form mutually hostile groups. In *On Aggression*, Konrad Lorenz, the great authority on animal behaviour, writes as follows:

> *Militant enthusiasm can be elicited, with the*
> *predictability of a reflex, when the following*
> *environmental situations arise. First of all, a social unit*
> *with which the subject identifies himself must appear to*
> *be threatened by some danger from outside. That which*

*is threatened may be a concrete group of people, the family
or a little community of close friends, or else it may be
a larger social unit held together and symbolised by its
own specific social norms and rites. As the latter assume
the character of autonomous values . . . they can, quite
by themselves, represent the object in whose defence
militant enthusiasm can be elicited. From all this it
follows that this response can be brought into play in
the service of extremely different objects, ranging from
the sports club to the nation, or from the most obsolete
mannerisms or ceremonials to the ideal of scientific
truth or the incorruptibility of justice.*

*A second key stimulus . . . is the presence of a hateful
enemy from whom the threat to the above 'values'
emanates . . . This enemy may be of a concrete or of an
abstract nature . . . , 'the' Jews, Huns, Boches,
Tyrants, . . . world capitalism, bolshevism, fascism and
any other kind of ism . . . A third factor contributing
to the environmental situation eliciting the response is
an inspiring leader figure. Even the most emphatically
antifascistic ideologies apparently cannot do without it,
as the giant pictures of leaders displayed by all kinds
of political parties prove clearly enough . . . A fourth,
and perhaps the most important prerequisite for the full
eliciting of militant enthusiasm is the presence of many
other individuals all agitated by the same emotion.*[2]

It seems that in order to evoke militant enthusiasm,
four things are needed: a group of persons, a cause, a
leader, and an enemy. We are apparently so constituted
that, if these are not provided for us, we are apt to invent
them; any cause, however absurd, any leader, however
wicked or stupid, will be better than none.[3] (The leader,
indeed, is only too likely to be wicked or stupid, since
otherwise he will be apt to be tormented by doubt about
the cause or about the propriety of his own leadership,
which will make him the less emotionally satisfying as a
leader.) Some people have, of course, been more noble or

more farsighted or both than this would suggest in their
choice of leader, cause and community. The Buddhist
maxim 'To the Buddha for refuge I go; to the Dharma for
refuge I go; to the Samgha for refuge I go'[4] perfectly
illustrates the point.

Now many sociologists and anthropologists strongly
contest the application by Konrad Lorenz of morals drawn
from animal behaviour to human beings, which is the
main topic of *On Aggression*. But I do not think that they
would generally be inclined to disagree with the judgement that we human beings *as a matter of fact* are prone
to militant enthusiasm, whether in good causes or in bad,
and that these are the circumstances which most conduce
to their indulgence of it. What they would be likely to
disagree with is the *explanation* in terms of factors common
to human beings and other animals. And it is the fact,
and the moral and political problems which it sets, which
is at issue here, and not the explanation.

Just suppose for a moment that there existed an
accredited community, imposing enough to inspire a loyalty which may cut national and class enthusiasm down
to size, which in fact demands the first loyalty of human
beings; a leader bearing signs of the highest possible
moral authority, of a character which is such as to attract
people's affections, control their aggressions, and hearten
their puny moral efforts to the highest degree; the cause
the advancement of the good as such, which overrides
the lesser and mutually conflicting 'goods' which are constituted by the interests of single individuals and of the
racial, social and economic groups of which they are members; the enemy only evil as such, and not the people who
are its victims and dupes. Might not the provision of such
a community, cause and leader plausibly be reckoned to
be the practical solution to that aspect at least of moral
evil on which the tendency to militant enthusiasm so
characteristic of human beings has a bearing?

The nature of the leader is a matter to which it is worth
giving some attention; he or she must be good, to be sure;

but mere goodness, which unfortunately is notoriously dull, is demonstrably insufficient to engage people's emotions in the moral struggle, beset as they are with myriad temptations to capitulate. If a person genuinely tries to be good, after all, she will not only be subject to painful conflict within herself, but will be at odds with powerful groups within society. What kind of leader could give her the heart confidently to apply herself to the struggle? In Mircea Eliade's *Patterns of Comparative Religion*[5] there is described a phenomenon which is characteristic of 'primitive' religion in almost all parts of the world. On the one hand there is belief in a remote Creator who has made all that exists, and is the original promulgator of the moral law. On the other hand, there is much more palpable religious involvement with a more intimate, concrete or dramatic type of god, demigod or hero, who is apt to be the focus of attention in the cultus. The story of this being's adventures is told and re-told, and his fate symbolically shared through rituals of participation. Here again there seems to be posed a very practical problem, the working-out of which may be seen in the annals and prophetic oracles of the Old Testament. The Israelite prophets jealously defended the honour of the one creator God; but the religious needs of their contemporaries were much more satisfactorily catered for by the various fertility gods and godlings. In the neighbouring cultures of Egypt and Mesopotamia the need for something concrete was met by the sacral kingship;[6] in Israel, again, such tendencies were in sharp contrast to loyalty to Yahweh as understood by the prophets.

As we have already seen, the study of comparative religion may well suggest conclusions consistent with these speculations; Zaehner writes of a 'hunger for an incarnate God'[7] which seems to express itself in the most unpromising religious environments. Just suppose that someone really claimed to be the unique 'son of God', and lived a life which made such a claim not obviously absurd; might not this be the ideal way of harnessing

militant enthusiasm in the service of the good, particularly
if he or she were the leader *of* the community, *for* the
cause, *against* the enemy I mentioned earlier? It would do
so presumably even more effectively if the history of this
person were closely analogous in the relevant respects to
the myths which human beings have always been prone
to construct about their cult-heroes; and if he or she had
himself or herself instituted a rite by which his or her
own fate might be applied and shared by votaries. The
story of the typical cult-hero or demigod, which is found
in various guises all over the world, has been summed
up as follows:

> *improbable origin, divine father, hazardous birth, rescue
> in the nick of time, precocious development . . . ,
> miraculous deeds, a tragic, early, and symbolically
> significant manner of death, post-mortem effects
> (reappearances, signs and marvels, etc.).*[8]

It does not need any remarkable powers of detection to see
that these elements occur in the New Testament narratives
about Jesus. If these narratives are historical, it does not
seem unnatural to see in them a historical key to a lock
constituted by the religious consciousness of humankind.
As to the institution of a rite—few propositions about the
historical Jesus seem more certain than that he did insti-
tute a rite whose reference was to himself.

If the manner of the atonement is rightly to be envisaged in the way that I have described, it is not difficult
to see the scope and limits of the traditional theories. The
living of the archetypal myth, as one might easily infer
even from the stories of James Bond and Philip Marlowe,
necessarily involves the undergoing of agony before
fulfilment, humiliation before glory. For God's very self
to be tormented and humiliated on humanity's behalf, so
that the tendency to sin should be effectively counter-
acted, is indeed for a great price to be paid; that the
payment of the price fulfils those desires and needs within

the human heart which otherwise tend to evil gives some appropriateness to the notion that it is to the Devil that God pays a ransom for humankind. Since God has acted in such a way that the predisposition to evil is or can be baulked, it is even more reasonable to say that God has won in Christ a victory over the powers of evil, that Satan is fallen like lightning from heaven, that the dragon has been defeated at last.[9] It is also evident that, by his obedience to the will of the Father, the Son has set an example to all humankind. The atonement is substitutionary in that, had the God-man not endured the anguish of living the archetypal myth, we ourselves would have been bound for the individual and collective misery which is the necessary result of sin. But it is not 'substitutionary' in a sense to which the kind of rational and moral objections mentioned at the beginning of this chapter are at all applicable. Thus it may easily be seen that, on the view of the atonement which I have sketched, none of the traditional theories of the atonement is very wide of the mark, though all of them are in need of the kind of explication and clarification which have only become fully possible with the advances in religious and social science which have come about in our own time.

All these points might be conceded, and the objection still made that the doctrine of the incarnation, which implies that one and the same being is really both God and man, is incoherent. Is not to be God to be unrestricted in knowledge and in power, while to be man is to be very limited in both these respects? Are not attributes essential to divinity thus incompatible with attributes essential to humanity?[10] Now a very large number of suppositions, like those of the reality of matter or of time, or the objectivity of goodness, have been confidently declared by philosophers to be incoherent; but the successors of these philosophers have commonly made light of such declarations. This fact might put orthodox believers on their guard when similar suggestions are made about the incarnation. Can we grasp, however inadequately, what a union of divine and human natures in one person might amount to? Other human persons, it has been suggested, through the whole of their intellectual and moral life, are implicitly directed, whether they know it or not, towards direct apprehension of the unrestricted understanding and infinite love which is God. Christ as man had this direct apprehension from the first; the whole of his life was directed towards expression by word and deed of this apprehension of the nature of God and how it stood with human beings in relation to God, in terms appropriate to the historical milieu within which he lived. Would this not fit quite neatly with what we find in the gospel narratives, assuming that they are at least in their main outlines historically reliable; as well as with the classical Christological formula worked out at the Council of Chalcedon that Christ is one 'person' in two 'natures', a human and a divine? Christ as God knew the Father as the Father knows himself; the life of Christ as man will have been an expression of this knowledge through the medium of the life of a human being amongst human beings. The apprehension of divinity possessed by Christ as human is one of which we may grasp some remote analogy through the words and writings of the mystics.[11]

I have tried to sketch a case for the traditional Christian doctrines of the incarnation and the atonement, and have covered a good deal of ground in doing so. It is time for me to summarize what I have attempted to do. To defend the doctrine, I suggested, one must explain how it could be relevant to the human situation. I have tried to bring out how consideration of certain facts about society and politics, about the history of religions, and about the human psyche, all bring out what Catholic theologians have called the *convenientia* of the incarnation; how the provision of a divine and human leader, who founded a community which demands our primary loyalty, would tend to harness our emotions and our aggressive tendencies in such a way as to make them available for the pursuit of truth and goodness, and for the struggle against evil and falsehood. If the leader were to have lived the archetypal myth of the hero, and instituted a rite through which his followers might identify with him and symbolically share his fate, that would be so much the better. At this rate one can see the point of the saying of Jesus to his disciples, 'Blessed are the eyes which see the things which you see: for I tell you, that many prophets and kings desired to see the things which you see, and saw them not; and to hear the things which you hear, and heard them not'.[12]

It is often maintained that insistence on the uniqueness of Christianity is bound to issue in a dismissive or hostile attitude to other religions. Now it is worth remembering that *whatever* is unequivocally affirmed, it is implied that *someone* may be mistaken. A religious belief assented to by all human beings of good will, or even all human beings of good will who could plausibly be called religious, is a religious belief without any content. If it is argued that belief in Christ is a stumbling-block to Jews and Muslims, it may be retorted that belief in God is equally a stumbling-block to Theravada Buddhists and Marxists. But it still remains that Christians have an immense amount to learn from Buddhists about the ultimate fruitlessness of selfishness and of sensual enjoyment; from Taoists about the natural law within human beings to which they ought to conform; from Confucians about the decent ordering of human society and proper respect for traditions; from Marxists about zeal for realizing justice on earth; from Jews about steadfastness and patience through suffering; from Muslims about the majesty, sovereignty, and immediate active presence of God; from Advaitin Hindus about God's intimate presence at the depths of ourselves; from Vaishnavite Hindus about the mystery[13] of God's incarnation; and so on. Confronted with the devoted lives of some persons of other religions, Christians may well feel that they are far nearer to the God revealed in Christ than most of those who have the special privilege of acknowledging him explicitly.

Notes

1 Examples would be John Hick and Maurice Wiles, as exemplified in their contributions to *The Myth of God Incarnate*, ed. Hick (London, 1977).
2 K. Lorenz, *On Aggression* (London, 1966), pp. 234ff.
3 See the alarming analogy drawn by Lorenz between man and a species of fish: Lorenz, op. cit., p. 125.
4 See E. Conze, *Buddhist Scriptures* (Harmondsworth, 1959), p. 182.
5 M. Eliade, *Patterns in Comparative Religion* (Cleveland, 1963), p. 109 and passim.
6 See the chapter on the sacral kingship in E. O. James, *The Ancient Gods* (New York, 1964).
7 R. C. Zaehner, *Concordant Discord* (London, 1970), p. 443.
8 C. G. Jung, *Psychology and Religion (Collected Works*, vol. XI; London, 1958), pp. 154ff.
9 Luke 10:18; Revelation 12:8; 17:14.
10 On the knowledge of Christ, see B. J. F. Lonergan, *De Verbo Incarnato* (Rome, 1964).
11 Luke 10:23–4.
12 Matthew 13:17; Luke 10:4.
13 It may be worth noting that by 'mystery' I mean an alleged fact which is puzzling to the intellect but very fascinating and emotionally moving; *not* a contradiction sententiously expressed.

F O U R

Christian belief and historical criticism

'What you have shown, at best, is that *if* God in Christ had actually spoken and acted in the manner described, it *would* have been appropriate to the human condition. But unfortunately for you, in the light of modern scholarship, we no longer have adequate grounds for believing that God really did so. The doctrine of the incarnation, of the divinity of Jesus Christ, implies certain things about the words, acts, and attitude towards himself, of the historical Jesus, which can now be demonstrated to be false beyond reasonable doubt.'

I quote from an article in the London *Times* by a well-known contemporary theologian. The 'revolution in examining the records of the past' which has been 'active steadily for the last 200 years' has had 'quite as far-reaching an effect on the study of the Bible as on any other part of historical study'. However, 'this revolution has had amazingly little effect upon the people in this country who use the Bible more than anybody else—the clergy and the faithful of all denominations'. The application of the moral to the gospel of John seems of special significance.

This is a litmus-paper test for preachers and expositors. If you can convince yourself that Jesus really did go round

*Galilee and Jerusalem saying such things as 'I am the
resurrection and the life', 'Which of you convinceth me
of sin?', and 'I and the Father are one', then of course
you can preserve a conventional view of Christianity.
But if, following the current of modern scholarship, you
come to the conclusion that this is incredible, what is
to be said in the pulpit, what is to be taught to the
faithful? . . . To commit oneself to the conclusion that
the Fourth Gospel is not, generally speaking, a record
of the words and deeds of Jesus of Nazareth, but a
profound and invaluable interpretation of his significance
written about the end of the first century A.D., is
indeed to call for a drastic re-examination of Christian
doctrine.*[1]

Do the results of modern Biblical study make it reasonable
to abandon Christianity? Are they more or less inconclus-
ive in this respect? Or do they perhaps enable Christianity
to be re-affirmed with additional forcefulness and conviction? The crucial area for investigation here seems to be
that into the historical Jesus. Is he roughly what traditional
Christianity presupposes that he is? If he is not, what
difference does this make to the contemporary Christian
believer, and why?

I shall outline five possibilities as to the nature of the
historical Jesus, and as to the relation of his words, his
actions and his self-consciousness to what we are told by
the gospels. I shall then consider some of the developments of contemporary scholarship in relation to these
possibilities.

(1) The words and deeds attributed to Jesus by the
evangelists are almost entirely mythical or legendary. A
few reputable scholars, as well as brilliant eccentrics like
John Allegro, have continued to hold this view until very
recent times; but though it had a certain vogue at the
end of the nineteenth and the beginning of the twentieth
century, it is by now very much a minority opinion. That

Christianity, except perhaps in some very attenuated form, is inconsistent with it, seems obvious enough.

(2) Jesus preached a message about the fatherhood of God and the universal brotherhood and sisterhood of humanity; but said and did nothing which alleged or implied any unique status for himself. I shall call this position 'the liberal Protestant view of Jesus', since I shall have occasion to refer to it a good deal. It has features which make it attractive to a great many people. It clearly enables its proponent to sit loose to the question of whether Jesus performed miracles, which lets her off some awkward scientific and philosophical problems. It also allows her to avoid what may be felt to be the moral and psychological scandal of a man making for himself the claims which Jesus must have made, if some strata of the gospels are to be regarded as historical. Also, what is specially attractive in these ecumenical days, it removes a central difficulty for Christians in their relations with Jews, Muslims, and many Hindus, who, while they share the Christian belief in God, find the doctrine of Christ's uniqueness a stumbling-block. On all these counts one can see the appeal of the view which regards those aspects of the gospels to which I have alluded as expressive rather of what Jesus' followers found that he meant *to them*, than of what he thought or said about *himself*.

(3) Jesus said and did things which implied his unique status in relation to God and to the rest of humankind; our gospels have largely changed the terms in which he did this.

(4) The terms in which Jesus expressed his consciousness of his unique status have been preserved fairly faithfully by the writers of the first three gospels; but not by the writer of the fourth gospel.

(5) Jesus' character, self-consciousness, and manner of speaking and acting have on the whole been preserved for us by the four gospels.

Of these five possibilities, I should say that the first and the second are clearly incompatible with traditional

Christianity, and that the third is at best questionably compatible with it; there may be some difficulty even about the fourth. But at least if the historical Jesus said and did nothing from which his consciousness of unique status would be a natural inference, the historical requirements of traditional Christianity are not fulfilled.[2] Christians have always presupposed that the picture of Jesus which we get from the gospels is at least roughly accurate; and it is difficult to see how Christianity could survive abandonment of this assumption except in a radically attenuated form. Now a very wide range of opinions as to the historical reliability of the gospels are held by serious scholars. Yet I think it can safely be said that the tide of scholarship, quite apart from the *Zeitgeist*, has set pretty heavily in opposition to the second position which I have called 'the liberal Protestant view of Jesus'. Subsequent research has on the whole confirmed the point forcefully argued by Albert Schweitzer at the beginning of the present century, that there are no consistent and objective principles of criticism, where the desired conclusions are not allowed more or less surreptitiously to dictate the method, whereby one can extract the liberal Protestant view of Jesus from the gospel narratives. Unfortunately there is no area of historical inquiry where there is greater danger that a historian's objectivity will be distorted by what she wishes or fears to find.

Now it is obvious that Christ's consciousness of his unique status, which differentiates our third and subsequent positions from the liberal Protestant view of Jesus, is put forward with especial clarity by the fourth gospel. It is thus inevitable that there should have been an alliance between the liberal Protestant view of Jesus on the one hand, and on the other hand a scholarly tendency to see the synoptic gospels as theologically garnished history, the fourth gospel as more or less pure theology; and the alliance has been an influential one right up to the present time. However, there have been two important scholarly developments, largely independent of one another, during the course of the present century, which have tended to subvert the alliance. One is the tendency to interpret the synoptic gospels themselves in a more Johannine way; the other a renewed appreciation of the historical value of the fourth gospel itself.

The manner in which theological considerations affected the formation of the material which we find in the synoptic gospels has been especially emphasized by the so-called form-critics. The natural application of form-criticism, which teases out the tendencies which affect the transmission of oral material, is to literature which existed long before it was committed to writing, like the Icelandic Eddas and much of the Hebrew scriptures. The method was first applied to the synoptic gospels in the early 1920s. While the best known of the form-critics, Rudolf Bultmann, came to very sceptical conclusions as to the historical reliability of the gospels, it is worth pointing out that acceptance of the validity of the method itself in no way commits one to these conclusions. One may grant that the primitive Christian community selected and shaped its memories of Jesus in the manner envisaged, without admitting that any considerable amount of falsification, either deliberate or inadvertent, was involved.[3] Also, it seems no less true of the form-critics than of their predecessors, that theological assumptions have been too inclined to dictate the result of historical investigation. With Bultmann, in particular, there appears to be a suspicious collusion between the sceptical results of the investigations of the historian, and the philosophical theologian's conception of faith as exclusively a matter of authentic existence here and now, which the results of historical investigation cannot conceivably confirm or impugn.[4]

The Riddle of the New Testament, which was published in the early 1930s, is in effect an onslaught on our second position, the liberal Protestant view of Jesus, from the point of view of the fourth. It has worn very well; I think because it combines sound scholarship with theological insight to a degree which in my experience is very rare.[5] It illustrates the manner in which an objective scrutiny of the first three gospels against their contemporary background may well lead a scholar to interpret their teaching in a curiously Johannine way, even when he does not regard the fourth gospel itself as historically reliable. The authors bring out how not only the synoptic evangelists themselves, but the whole tradition behind them, regard Jesus' words and deeds as fulfilling prophecies in the Hebrew scriptures of the Messianic age. For example, when John the Baptist is said to have sent messengers from prison asking Jesus whether he was indeed 'he that should come', they are sent back to tell John about Jesus' cures of the blind, the deaf and the lepers; and it is implied that these acts of his constitute the fulfilment of prophecy.[6] Just the same applies to the nature-miracles, as comes out very vividly at the end of the Marcan account of the stilling of the storm: 'Who is this, that the wind and the sea obey him?' In the background is the reference by the Psalmist to God who stills the raging of the sea.[7] The two feedings of the multitude, significantly set 'in a desert place', recall the miraculous feeding of the Israelites on the way to the Promised Land, and the expectation, probably based on this, of a great feast in the Messianic age at which all will be filled.[8] The point of the difficult story of the cursing of the barren fig-tree, whether it was originally a miracle[9] or a parable[10] or both, is the rejection of Israel. The primary significance of all these miracle stories, in the mind both of the evangelists themselves and the bearers of the traditions which they transmitted, is 'the person of Christ and the action of God . . . Who is this who has authority to reject Israel? Who is this who has authority to forgive sin? Who is this who is stronger than the devil and deprives him of his retinue of human slaves?' Even if one were to suppose that all the miracle-stories are transformed parables, the point at issue, the messianic claim of Jesus, would still remain.[11]

The exponents of the liberal Protestant view of Jesus

have been inclined to see in the parables themselves general lessons of a moral and spiritual nature—the parable of the talents extolling the virtue of thrift, the Good Samaritan that of helpfulness, the story of the Pharisee and the Publican that of humility, and so on.[12] Certainly it would be a serious distortion of the gospels to go so far as to deny the presence of these general moral lessons; but the centre of attention is definitely elsewhere. In this case as well, it is the background in the Hebrew scriptures which supplies the crucial key. There are many parables about sowing and reaping attributed to Jesus; for example, he spoke of seed which grows by itself, of a tiny seed which grows into a large tree,[13] and of wheat which grows up mixed with weeds until the harvest.[14] But the prophet Hosea had pictured the final establishment of Israel as a sowing;[15] and in the books of Isaiah and Jeremiah the good age to come is seen in terms of a divine sowing and a fruitful field.[16] Other prophecies envisage as a harvest the divine visitation of wrath and judgement;[17] though for one Psalmist the harvest is a symbol of joy and deliverance.[18]

To minds saturated in the Hebrew scriptures, the interpretation of these words of Jesus about the harvest as a claim to be the Messiah, and to be bringing in the messianic age, would have been the inevitable one.

> *Other parables betray the same careful choice of simile and metaphor. More than once Isaiah had referred to Israel as God's vineyard. The parables of the wedding-feast and of the waiting of the virgins for the bridegroom are foreshadowed in the betrothing of Israel to God and the great feast of the coming age typified by the manna in the wilderness.*[19]

What had long been prefigured and foretold, was said and shown by Jesus to be taking place there and then.[20] The point of Jesus' attitude to the Sabbath, again, was not merely humanitarian concern, or a polemic against that kill-joy attitude to the Sabbath which was evidently deplored by the most articulate Jewish thought at the time—though these elements are certainly present; but rather the ushering-in of the messianic age of which the Jewish sabbath had been an anticipation.[21]

We know the beliefs of the primitive Church directly from the documents which constitute the New Testament; we know Jesus himself only indirectly through these beliefs. This is why, in assessment of the extent of our knowledge of him as an actual historical individual, we have to use the methods of historical criticism. Two possibilities have to be weighed against one another. 'Did the life and death of Jesus of Nazareth control the life of the primitive Church? Or was his life and death submerged by a piety and faith wholly beyond his horizon?'[22] It may be concluded, from what has been said, that the former is the case; that there is a single basic Christology which is present as an organizing principle throughout all the strata of the material, to the effect that Jesus is the promised Messiah who has inaugurated the Kingdom of God by his coming. Every scrap of relevant evidence tells against the latter possibility, which would imply that the material existed at some time apart from the Christology, and that the Christology was forced onto material which was originally independent of it.[23]

The authors of *The Riddle of the New Testament* suggest that, if their main argument is correct, the heat is to a large extent taken out of the questions of the apostolic authorship of the fourth gospel, and its historicity. For it is by no means the case that, if these are denied, the liberal Protestant view of Jesus is vindicated against the traditional and orthodox one; since the conception of Jesus which undergirds and determines the material of the synoptic gospels is really just as discrepant with the liberal Protestant view of Jesus as is the picture presented by the fourth gospel. For that picture, though, as the authors of *The Riddle of the New Testament* believed, it is largely unhistorical in detail, amounts in the end to much the same thing as is presupposed throughout the other gospels.[24]

However, the case for the substantial historicity of the fourth gospel is now a great deal stronger than it was in the 1930s. It used to be very widely accepted, by authorities working in the field, that John is a work which as a whole reflects a Hellenistic milieu of the late first or even early second century CE. But evidence has been steadily mounting against this view over the last 50 years. As early as 1922, C. F. Burney had published a book which argued that John was originally written in Aramaic. It would be out of place to go into the details of the discussion here— it turns on alleged mistranslations, Aramaic quirks of syntax in the Greek, and so on. However, while Burney's extreme view has not on the whole commended itself to scholars, one may say that the presence of a strong Aramaic undercurrent in the gospel, which the theory of its Hellenistic origin as a whole has at least to take account of, may now be taken as established.[25]

Once authorship of the fourth gospel by John the son of Zebedee had largely been abandoned by the critics, the consensus was that it presupposed the synoptics, and amounted to an interpretation of their account of Jesus which reflected the theology and sacramental practice of the Church around the end of the first century. In particular, it was very widely held that the author knew the gospel of Mark, and probably that of Luke as well; and that what he wrote was by way of commentary or corrective. But for the last fifty years or so, somewhat cogent arguments have been put forward for the complete independence of the gospel of John.[26] Thus in sections of the gospels of Mark and John which apparently refer to the same event, it may be shown time and time again that words which are identical in the two accounts are just those which would naturally be retained in divergent oral traditions of the same occurrence; while the differences would be impossible to account for if the author of John knew the gospel of Mark.[27] It has been added that if, as

on the commonly-accepted account of the relation
between the synoptic gospels, the authors of the gospels
of Matthew and Luke both knew the gospel of Mark,
there is a case for putting the composition of the Gospel
of John before that of those of Matthew or Luke, when
knowledge of the gospel of Mark must have been widespread in the Church.[28]

In opposition to an earlier tendency to see the topogra-
phy of the fourth gospel as rather symbolical than literal,
the accuracy of its many topographical details has tended
to be confirmed by recent archaeological investigation.
Thus the 'pavement' (*lithostrōton*) mentioned in John 19:13
has been excavated; and more or less tentative identifi-
cations, which together have rather an impressive effect,
have been made of other sites. Sometimes, again, when
parallel passages in the gospel of John and the synoptics
are compared according to the methods evolved by the
form critics, and questions of relative priority are not
begged, the material underlying the Johannine account
seems more primitive than that underlying the synoptic
account. For example, C. H. Dodd points out that in the
case of the episode of the cleansing of the Temple, John
has preserved a form of a kind recognized as primitive
by the form critics, while Mark has disintegrated it.[29]

The Dead Sea Scrolls, discovered at Qumran in 1947,
provide an account of the beliefs and practices of a Jewish
sect as just about the time of the life of Jesus. It was thus
only to be expected that they would be of considerable
significance for New Testament studies; but what was
surprising was the special light which they shed on the
discourses of Jesus as reported in the gospel of John.
Particularly striking is the common form of the dualism
found in the Qumran *Manual of Discipline* and in the
words of Jesus according to John, with their stress on
the contrast between light and darkness, truth and falsehood.[30] As Raymond Brown has put it

. . . much of the same vocabulary, mentality, and

theological outlook found in John is found also at Qumran both before and during Christ's time. A real Palestinian background has been discovered against which the Jesus of John can plausibly be pictured.[31]

The late great scholar C. H. Dodd, to whose influence the 'new look' at the fourth gospel is very deeply indebted, claimed that the course taken by the nineteenth-century 'quest of the historical Jesus' proved that a severe concentration on the synoptic record, to the exclusion of the Johannine, leads to 'an impoverished, a one-sided, and finally an incredible view of the facts'.[32] In the case of Jesus' prediction of his death and what was to follow it, Dodd thought that the Johannine vagueness was likely to be original, the comparative precision in the synoptic accounts a later development. Again, given the situation in which the early Church found herself in relation to the Roman empire, it is easier to believe that the synoptics have softened the political overtones of the trial of Jesus, than that John has heightened them. There are passages where John appears to clarify points left obscure by the synoptics; for example, Peter's confession, which comes quite abruptly in the synoptics, is introduced naturally by an account of many desertions by followers of Jesus in the gospel of John. Similarly, the abrupt disappearance into solitude by Jesus after the feeding of the multitude is explained by John; Jesus knew that otherwise he would be set up as a political leader.

As to the Johannine discourses and dialogues, Dodd remarked that material closely related to the synoptic tradition was so closely embedded in them as to be apparently inseparable from the argument of which they form part. And in examining parallels in the gospel of John to synoptic sayings, one is sometimes brought to the heart of Johannine theology. The saying about the reciprocal knowledge of Father and Son, transmitted in one of the most primitive strata of the synoptic tradition,[33] is the most striking example of this, but by no means the only one. Again, passages in John with no synoptic parallel, and with thoroughly Johannine doctrine, are sometimes framed in apparently traditional forms—for example, the sayings about the grain of wheat and the wind.[34]

For all the striking differences between the words of Jesus as given in the synoptics and by John, it has been pointed out that there is an underlying unity of symbolism and its application which can more plausibly be attributed to Jesus himself than to the ingenuity, however extraordinary, of the fourth evangelist. Thus the analogies of light, of shepherd and sheep, of wheat and harvest, are applied in the gospels to the disciples, the Kingdom of God, and to Jesus himself; while the third application is most obviously to the fore in John, it is often strongly hinted at in the synoptics.[35] Sometimes John seems to provide an answer to what is a mere puzzle on the synoptic account, as in the case of the sequence of events in the Upper Room. In the gospels of Mark and Matthew, Jesus announces his betrayal and then, as it were out of the blue, identifies samples of bread and wine as his body and blood. Luke takes the matter a little further, but not much. But in the gospel of John, there is a much fuller account, with a discourse to interpret its significance; and, earlier in the gospel, a discourse on Jesus as the bread of life, through which 'the feeding of the five thousand is . . . seen to point to Jesus as the ultimate answer to man's hunger'.[36] Without some such background, the institution of the Eucharist as recorded in the synoptics is surely itself virtually unintelligible.

Oscar Cullmann has suggested that Jesus himself may well be supposed to have spoken rather differently to those whose background was orthodox Judaism on the one hand, and those who had sectarian connections on the other; and he adds that this difference may account for many of the well-known contrasts between his teaching as recorded in the synoptics and in John. That Jesus occasionally spoke in a manner rather different from the usual one represented in the synoptics is confirmed by at least one well-attested saying, which has already been cited as preserved by the synoptic tradition itself. It is evident from the book of Acts that there existed from the early days of the Church, in the 'deacons', an important group of Christian missionaries who were at least to some degree independent of the Twelve, and it seems quite likely that this group already existed during the ministry of Jesus.[37] And there are strong hints in the speech of Stephen reported in Acts that he may have been associated with the circle from which the fourth gospel later emanated; Stephen shares with John, and with many circles of heterodox Judaism, his opposition to the Temple, though there is no trace in the speech of John's conception of Christ as the new Temple.

The encounter of Jesus with the Samaritan woman in the fourth chapter of the gospel of John, where again the matter of the Temple is at issue, suggests a close connection between the Johannine circle and the Samaritan mission in the early Church; and we know from Acts that the deacons were active in Samaria. That the Samaritan mission was inaugurated before the crucifixion is corroborated by evidence in the synoptic gospels of Jesus' special fondness for Samaritans, by the special mention of Samaria in the mission charge at the beginning of Acts, and by the rapid success of the mission in the period immediately after the death of Jesus.[38] It may be added that Jesus' references to the 'Son of Man', abundantly attested by the synoptic gospels as well as the fourth gospel, is a witness to his association with esoteric Judaism.[39] Cullmann's thesis is controversial; but it does hint at a possible solution to the problem of the differences between the first three gospels and the fourth, other than that the latter is basically unhistorical.

The most striking recent vindication of John as historically reliable is due to J. A. T. Robinson.[40] A distinguished New Testament archaeologist wrote to Robinson as follows, in the course of congratulating him on his work: 'I have long felt that John is early and trustworthy and is to be taken seriously in his historical as well as theological sense and not to be relegated to a secondary position after the Synoptics.'[41] Robinson points out that the synoptics and John are more similar to one another than is often acknowledged.[42] Thus some parallels in John to the synoptics look like translations of the same Aramaic words;[43] and though John obviously does not contain full-scale parables in the manner of the synoptics, it remains that there are little parables to be unearthed in that gospel.[44] According to both the synoptic and the Johannine traditions, Jesus was in the habit of employing synonymous, antithetical, and climactic parallelism in his speech. Clearly the poetic form of this material does not of itself prove it to represent the actual words of Jesus; but we know from the synoptics that Jesus had this gift, and we do not know that the fourth evangelist had it.[45] As is remarked by the Aramaic scholar Matthew Black, the poetical form of the Johannine discourses, together with their rabbinical flavour, does 'not discourage the belief that much more of the ipsissima verba [of Jesus] may have been preserved in the fourth gospel . . . than we have dared believe possible for many years'.[46]

The Dead Sea Scrolls demonstrate that 'mystical, pregnostic' language of the Johannine kind, and the more apocalyptic manner which one associates with the synoptics, could coexist in the same individual—as indeed we know in any case from the writings of St Paul; one might infer, in accordance with W. H. Brownlee's suggestion, that 'the two types of vocabulary belonged authentically to Jesus, with a polarization of the two elements taking place in the different Gospel traditions'.[47] It is obvious enough that the divine nature and heavenly origin of Jesus are more strongly emphasized in John than in the synoptics; but it does not immediately follow from this that the Johannine Jesus is less human. Indeed, 'the marks of emotional strain and psychic disturbance are quite as evident in John as they are in Mark'.[48] In some respects John may actually be the more 'primitive'; Robinson

judges, following C. H. Dodd, that 'the Johannine eschatology represents a tradition that had never undergone
the process of increasing apocalypticization visible in the
synoptic tradition'.[49] Chronologically speaking, the synoptic material fits neatly into the Johannine framework,
while the converse by no means applies; and aspects of
the synoptic narrative actually become more intelligible
in the process.[50]

The view that the composition of the fourth gospel went
through a number of stages, and lasted over many years,
is by no means incompatible with overall[51] unity of
authorship; this scenario seems to me furthermore to con-
sort very well with what is known of ancient methods
of recording the lives and teachings of great men.[52] The
hypothesis of multiple authorship fits badly with the consistency of manner and style which is one of the most
striking features of the work, and appears confirmed by
detailed stylistic analysis. As Pierson Parker says, 'It looks
as though, if the author of the fourth gospel used docu-
mentary sources, he wrote them all himself'.[53]

It is fair to say that there are still many first-rate scholars
who continue to hold that the fourth gospel demonstrates
that the early Christians were more influenced by the
resurrection and the emergence of the Church than they
were by the actual teaching of Jesus.[54] Still, some good
scholars have always been convinced of the basic historicity of the fourth gospel, while others have come to be
converted recently by the gradual accumulation of evidence.[55] I conclude that the implications of traditional
Christian belief for Jesus' own conception of his person
and work, though they are often thought to be impugned
by objective historical investigation, in fact tend to be
confirmed by much of the latest research into the
gospels.[56]

For the incarnation to be true, in the classical Christian
sense, is nothing else than for the one Jesus Christ to be
at once really divine and really human, truly God and
truly man. The whole point of the Greek Councils from

Nicaea to Chalcedon, as I shall try to show, is to assert clearly and unequivocally the real divinity and the real humanity of the one individual Jesus Christ. The heresies of the early Church, so far as they have a bearing on Christology, nearly all amount to or imply a denial of this. That the New Testament taken as a whole teaches that Jesus was really a man is clear enough; not only did he look and behave like a man, but he could feel hungry and thirsty, and undergo grief and agonizing pain. What about his divinity? That explicit assertions of his divinity are very few is obvious enough; but one should not infer too readily from this that his divinity is not expressed more or less indirectly by the New Testament writings taken together. In fact, the New Testament witness to the divinity of Christ has all the allusiveness and complexity of symbolism of a mature Shakespeare play. How is this indirectness to be accounted for?

Jesus, as has been well said, could not have got up among the Jews and said 'I am God, strictly speaking', for the excellent reasons that they would have understood him to mean (to express the matter in the later terminology) 'I am God the Father', which would have been heretical by later standards; and because 'strictly speaking' is an expression which presupposes a technical precision in the use of concepts not available within the cultural milieu of that place and time.[57] But the fact remains that, in the writings of the New Testament, the conception of a divine being other than God the Father is brought out in a whole host of ways. That Jesus is at least in some sense, as against what the Patripassians claimed, other than God the Father, according to the consensus of New Testament writers, scarcely needs to be shown; Jesus is represented in all the gospels as praying to the Father, and even the passages with the most exalted Christology distinguish 'God' or 'God the Father' or 'the Father' as another than 'Jesus' or 'his Son' or 'the Son'. Yet Jesus forgives sins, as only the Father can do; he feeds the people in 'a desert place', as God did their fathers in the wilderness; he rules the sea, like the Lord as described by the Psalmist; he gives life to the dead as the Father does; he proclaims a new law, and inaugurates a new covenant. Jesus speaks with divine authority;[58] he has a knowledge of God unique among human beings; he expels demons with the finger of God; the prophetic 'day of the Lord' is his day, and the prophetic preparation of the way of the Lord is preparation of the way for him. To know him is to know the Father; all that belongs to the Father belongs to him; he is the equal of the Father. He is associated with God in the work of creation; is worthy along with God of the titles Alpha and Omega, beginning and end, first and last; and is the Word who was with God in the beginning.[59] The texts which directly assert or presuppose the divinity of Christ, which admittedly are few and arguably are late,[60] are thus by no means isolated or aberrant, but serve to make patent and unequivocal what is latent in the whole.

If the liberal Protestant view of Jesus is correct, all of these suggestions, and not merely the explicit statements of Christ's divinity, are to be regarded as secondary and derivative rather than arising more or less directly out of the words and deeds of the historical Jesus himself. In that case, there are excellent grounds for saying that the classical Christian doctrine of the incarnation is a distortion of what was originally proclaimed by Jesus and the first disciples. I have argued that, on the contrary, the doctrine of the incarnation is after all a reasonable conclusion from the New Testament evidence taken as a whole, and is not really weakened when this is subjected to the most stringent historical criticism.

The major Christian denominations appeal not only to Scripture, but to the Councils of the early Church, as determining what is central to their belief. What, it may be asked, is the relation between the New Testament and the Councils of the Church? What is the bearing on the mission and message of the gospel of the doctrines of the Trinity and the Person of Christ which the Church hammered out from the fourth to the sixth centuries? It will be an important part of my case that this matter is often seriously misunderstood, not just by ordinary people, but by professional theologians.

I will now try to express as clearly as I can the misgivings which many people feel about conciliar formulations of doctrine, both in themselves and in their relation to Scripture. In the New Testament, it may seem, one is confronted with a simple and splendid message, which is of immediate relevance to all human beings in all situations; and, as befits such a message, expressed in terms which all persons, not only scholars and intellectuals, can understand, at least in its essentials. As has rightly been said, it did not seem fitting for God to save people by abstract argument, which is something of which few are capable in any case; what God requires is conversion of the heart and will, contemplation of Jesus Christ as the New Testament presents him to us, the giving of ourselves to him and to the God revealed in him, and the re-orientation of our lives accordingly.

To move from the gospels to the ecumenical Councils is to move into a different and utterly alien world. Expressions of a metaphysical character like 'substance', 'nature' and 'hypostasis' abound; and everything which is of religious or human significance in the gospel seems to have been completely forgotten. Talk about 'substance' and the rest of it is not the language of worship or of repentance. Even if it be granted that the Fathers were settling issues which were genuinely Christian for their own time and place, it may seem that what they did cannot have the slightest relevance to the problems which press on Christians of our time and place. Why should we be in the least concerned with whether or not Jesus is 'consubstantial' with the Father, whatever that is; or whether he has two 'natures', whatever they are? We are rather disposed to wonder why Christian intellectuals should ever have exercised their minds over such pointless questions.[61]

Evidently we are dealing with a technical language; and before we dismiss too readily the Fathers' conclusions, it may be worthwhile to reflect a little on what technical languages are for. Apart from enabling their adepts to recognize one another as members of the same club, they do have the more useful and serious functions of clarifying problems which arise within a field, and expressing clearly and distinctly conclusions which have been reached within it. You can anticipate and explain a very wide range of phenomena by means of the technical terminology involved in Newton's laws of motion, or in the periodic table of chemical elements.

The fundamental mistake which is apt to be made about the Councils of the Church, I believe, is to suppose that they were adjudicating, for better or for worse, on matters of complicated and obscure metaphysical speculation. The Fathers did, as a matter of fact, go in for a good deal of metaphysical speculation in trying to come to terms with what they regarded as divine revelation in Scripture, some being influenced by Stoic materialism, others by Neoplatonism; but this is not what is *primarily* relevant to understanding what was going on in the Councils of the Church over the period with which we are concerned. What the Councils were trying to do in the first instance was to provide *answers* to *questions* which inevitably nag the attentive reader of the New Testament—all deriving from what is the question of all questions for Christians, who or what is Jesus Christ? What the questions were, and what the Fathers rightly or wrongly thought that the wrong answers to them were, is brought out with special clarity by the great heresies. How are the fact that Jesus was a real man on the one hand, and his unique relationship to God on the other, to be reconciled with one another?

It was maintained by some that Jesus was a mere man commissioned with a special task by God (Ebionism). At the other extreme, it was asserted that Jesus was simply identical with God the Father (Sabellianism or

Patripassianism). The Church at large rejected both of these positions, and, in the light of the New Testament, it is quite easy to see why. The former fails to do justice to what is said of Jesus Christ in the New Testament, especially in the gospel of John and the Pauline epistles. The latter goes against the clear distinction made by the writers, and apparently by Jesus himself, between 'the Son of Man' and 'God', between 'the Son' and 'the Father', between 'me' and 'my Father', and so on. A number of compromise positions were later suggested; Christ was human in appearance, but was really simply divine (Docetism); he had a human body, but not a human soul with real human thoughts and feelings (Apollinarism); he was the first created and highest among all creatures, but was called 'divine' only by courtesy (Arianism); the man Jesus and the divine Word of God were not strictly speaking one and the same being, but two distinct individuals intimately united in will and intention (Nestorianism).

The Church needed not only to reject these heresies themselves, but at the same time to meet the questions which the heretics were attempting to answer. It was explicitly against Arianism that the Council of Nicaea determined that Jesus Christ was 'consubstantial' with the Father. It is sometimes asserted or assumed that this term was taken over from contemporary Greek philosophy; but this is wrong as a matter of historical fact. Before the Council of Nicaea, the term was used to mean 'of the same stuff', being applicable for example to beds or tables made of the same material. The Fathers took this term over and used it in a technical way, rather as modern physicists have done with the term 'particle'; what they were using it *for* may be determined by a consideration of that Arian heresy which their use of the term was deliberately designed to exclude. The objection that the term was unscriptural was considered very carefully by the Fathers; in the end they set the objection aside, because biblical terminology did not enable them to state what they wanted to state, and exclude what they wanted to exclude, with enough precision. The Arians denied that the Son, our Lord Jesus Christ, was really and truly divine in the sense that the Father was. The Fathers of Nicaea wanted to say that he was really and truly divine; as such, consubstantial with the Father in respect of his divinity, as he is consubstantial with us in respect of his humanity.

What *is* it, in the light of these considerations, for A to be consubstantial with B? Two dogs are consubstantial in respect of their doghood, two horses in respect of their horsiness; but a dog and a horse are not consubstantial with one another in either of these respects. And, to take an example which is more germane to the case of Arianism, a cow which is only by courtesy a horse, merely deemed to be a horse perhaps for some legal or cultic reason, is not consubstantial with a real horse. To put the thing rather formally: suppose that X is a specimen of the type A, and that to be A is to have the qualities p, q, r and s; then Y will be consubstantial with X in respect to A-hood if and only if it also has the qualities p, q, r and s.

It may be objected that everything that I have said brings out the irrelevance of what the Fathers were doing for any religious concerns. What has all this to do with the God and Christ whom Christians worship, and to whom they dedicate their lives? Now it is true that this kind of talk has nothing *directly* to do with religion and devotion; but *indirectly* it has a very great deal to do with both. It has just as much to do with them as, for example, the discoveries of the bacteriologist in her laboratory have with the treatment of patients in a hospital for infectious diseases. Suppose you believe, for example, as Jews, Muslims and Christians are apt to do, that it is blasphemous to worship a being who is anything less than God. It follows from this that it is blasphemous to worship Jesus Christ if he is not really and truly God, that is to say, 'consubstantial' with the Father in the sense intended by the Fathers at Nicaea. So, if Christians are concerned with the worship of Jesus Christ, the matter *does* appear after all to be important, and indeed of the very greatest importance, for the Christian religion.

The Nicene formula amounts to a rule about what one is to say about the Son, in relation to what one is in the habit of saying about God the Father. It is technical talk, the purpose of which is to regulate and control talk which is more directly religious. To grasp this is to be in a position to see what the Fathers really did owe to Greek culture. As it has been well expressed, they did not so much take over Hellenic concepts, as avail themselves of a Hellenic technique.[62] The technique was that of abstraction, that of not merely talking about things, but talking about talk about things. The technique turned out to be not merely useful, but urgently necessary, when persons at once of greater intellectual sophistication, and of different culture, from those among whom the gospel was first proclaimed, started asking questions about faith in Jesus Christ, its meaning and implications.

Now the term 'consubstantial' was taken over by theologians to meet an emergency, that of the Arian heresy; but once the process had begun, for better or worse, of resorting to non-biblical terminology for the formulation of doctrine, there was no stopping it. No sooner had the question of the consubstantiality of the Son with the Father been settled, than a new question arose, of the consubstantiality of the Holy Spirit with the Father and the Son. And given that not only the Father was God, but that at least one other being distinct from the Father also was God, there was a pressing question of how it could be that there was not more than one God. The Fathers wished to hold, in order to do justice, as they thought, to what they read in the New Testament, both, with the Jews, that there was one God, and, in a manner which sounded like a concession to polytheism, that there was more than one who was God; that there were the Father, the Son, and the Holy Spirit, each distinct from the others, and each God, and yet that there was only one God.[63] To say that God was three 'persons' or 'hypostases' in one 'substance' did nothing more or less than assert these apparently contradictory propositions clearly and distinctly. 'Substance', and 'hypostasis' or 'person', in the context of these early Councils, are nothing more or less than whatever there is deemed to be one of, and whatever there are deemed to be three of, in God. They leave it open to later orthodox believers to conceive of God in a wide range of ways, provided only that the rule implicit in the formulation of the doctrine is adhered to.

Christians are told on good authority that new wine needs fresh wineskins.[64] The new life in Christ could not but involve, incidentally, a conceptual revolution, of which the foundation and the first stages are clearly to be discerned in the New Testament itself. The development went on long after the New Testament period, for reasons into which we have already gone. One may say that in general, when a radically new message has to be conveyed, at first language has to be used poetically and dramatically, simply because no other kind of conceptualization has had the opportunity to evolve; after a while, given the right environment, a technical language which sets out the content of the message with logical consistency, given that the message is not self-contradictory, is developed.[65] The Fathers were impelled to embark on this process of conceptual development and revision by particular pressing problems as they arose. The medieval scholastics strove to complete the process, to work out a fully systematic account, in which all apparent contradictions might be resolved, of the Christian revelation in relation to humanity and the world as then conceived. To refound, revise or recreate this achievement of theirs for our own time, given that Christianity as an informed and coherent account of the world and humanity's place in it is to survive at all, is the main task on the agenda of a contemporary Christian theology.

What was at issue in the doctrine that God is 'three persons in one substance', at least when it was first formulated, comes out beautifully in the story of how Athanas-

ius resolved the dispute between those who objected to
the phrase 'three hypostases' or persons, and those on the
other hand who objected to talk of 'one substance'. He
asked the former if they wanted to revive the heresy of
Sabellius, who had denied any real distinction between
the persons; and the latter whether they were tritheists
who believed in three gods. Each side was perfectly
astounded at the question put to them, grasped that the
formula amounted precisely to the exclusion of tritheism
at one extreme and Sabellianism on the other, and acknowledged their dispute as purely verbal. Those who
were bothered by the formula 'three persons' in fact acknowledged what was meant by the phrase, and the same
applied to those who had jibbed at the expression 'one
substance'. *How* the three could be distinct as persons, yet
one as God, was a problem left to later speculation; the
point of the doctrinal advance made was *that* they were
so.[66]

Just the same principles, it may easily be seen, apply to
the conciliar teaching on the person of Christ as to that
on the Trinity. A lot of time and ink is wasted on the
pseudo-problem of what the philosophical or metaphysical background is to the concepts 'person' and 'nature',
and in deploring the error of the Fathers in corrupting
the gospel message by imposing them on the faithful in
a formula which demanded their assent. But what is really
at issue is something much simpler and more straight-
forward than this. The term 'nature' or *phusis* certainly
had a philosophical background, for example in the work
of Aristotle; so, though to a lesser extent, did 'hypostasis',
in Stoic writers. However, this is not what is of primary
relevance. What *is* so relevant is the particular set of problems with which the Fathers were faced. The point of the
formula on which they finally fixed, 'one person in two
natures', appears luminously from the English title of a
famous modern work on Christology, Pannenberg's *Jesus,
God and Man*. Jesus is both God and man, and in that way
and to that extent two 'things'; but there was only one

Jesus who was the two 'things', God and man, human and divine. Similarly, Bruce Woodcock was both a boxing champion and a railway worker. It is obviously one thing to be a boxing champion, another to be a railway worker. But the fact remains that there were not two individuals, one of whom was the boxer, the other the railway worker; it was one and the same person, Bruce Woodcock, who was both.

If you take with full seriousness the proposition that it is *one and the same* (as Cyril of Alexandria so strenuously insisted) who is both really God and really man, you acknowledge exactly what is intended by the formula 'one person in two natures'. The school of Antioch were particularly concerned with stressing the divinity and the humanity, the school of Alexandria the unity of Christ; this tended to give rise to misunderstandings, quite apart from the compromises suggested by the heresies. Perhaps he didn't have human thoughts, feelings and desires (Apollinarism)? Perhaps there were two individuals, the eternal divine Word and the human Jesus, with a particularly intimate unity of thought and intention (Nestorianism)?[67] Against these positions, the Council of Chalcedon solemnly determined in effect that it was one and the same Jesus Christ who was really divine and really human, and in that sense had two natures. 'Person', in the context of this Council, is nothing more or less than the technical term for what there is one of, 'nature' for what there are two of, in Jesus Christ. Further determination of what was meant by each term was left to later thinkers.[68] Our own period, with its preoccupation with persons and personal relations, assuming that the term is not wholly equivocal as between the conciliar and the modern sense, may be expected to contribute a great deal more to the explication of the concept.[69]

It has been maintained that, while the modern Christian may still be committed to the fundamental Christian beliefs in the Trinity and the Incarnation, she cannot now affirm that God is three persons in one substance, or that

Christ is one person in two natures, without tearing her-self right out of the context of modern thought.[70] If what I have said is on the right lines, it may easily be seen that this claim is at least rather odd. So long as one believes in the doctrine of the Trinity at all, one cannot but believe that there are three of something in God; and, so far as the doctrinal context of the fourth and fifth centuries is concerned, 'person' is simply the term for what there are three of in God, 'substance' for what there is one of. And unless our hypothetical modern Christian wants to be some kind of polytheist (which is rare) or atheist (which is unusual) or Sabellian modalist, or unless she simply wants to deny the divinity of the Son or of the Holy Spirit (which seems rather common), then she can hardly but assent in effect to the formula in the sense in which it was intended. The case with the doctrine of the person and natures of Christ is even more clear-cut. Does the contemporary believer deny that Christ was divine? Does she deny that he was human? Does she deny that it is one and the same individual, Jesus Christ, who is at once divine and human? Perhaps she does, in which case she denies the doctrine of the incarnation; but given that she doesn't, then she accepts in effect, even if she denies it verbally, that Christ is one person in two natures.

In the aftermath of the Council of Chalcedon, it was determined that the human nature taken over by the divine Word was personless. Some contemporary theo-logians have inferred from this that Jesus Christ cannot be a human person; and rejecting this conclusion, in my opinion perfectly rightly, as intolerable, they have rejected the doctrine from which they inferred it.[71] But it does not seem to me that the conclusion, that Christ is not a real human person (at least in the modern sense), follows from the premise, that the humanity assumed by the divine Word was personless (*anhupostaton* as opposed to *enhupostaton*). I quote Anthony Hanson on the topic:

During my theological formation, I distinctly remember

> *being told that the Word of God, when he assumed*
> *human nature, assumed impersonal humanity; that Jesus*
> *Christ did not possess a human personality, that God*
> *became man in Jesus Christ, but did not become a man.*[72]

Now I concede that it is traditional orthodox Christian doctrine that the eternal Word of God 'assumed impersonal humanity'; but I do take issue with what is claimed in the passage cited to be implied by this. The point of the doctrine is that the Word of God did not take over a ready-made human person, as on the adoptionist or Nestorian view; but took over a set of properties by virtue of which he *became* truly a man, truly human, and thus certainly, in the modern sense of the terms, a real human person possessing a real human personality.

If, to make an extravagant supposition, I become a baker, I do not take a baker, but rather bakerhood, upon myself; that is, I acquire the diplomas, skills and means of production constitutive of being a baker. Another individual being, another person, does not come into existence when I become a baker. So it is, according to this aspect of traditional orthodox Christian doctrine, with the incarnation. When the man Jesus was conceived, it was not the individual person as such, who is none other than the eternal Word of God, who came into existence; rather this eternal Word first came to exist *as* a man. This after all is only the logical consequence of the belief that he whom the first disciples knew as a man among men really was none other than the eternal Word of God. I strongly agree with Professor Hanson that it is both absurd and unchristian to suppose that 'Jesus Christ did not possess a human personality, that God became man in Jesus Christ, but did not become *a* man'; and that if traditional orthodoxy had such consequences, that would be a substantial point against it. But I do not believe that it has such consequences, or even that they are consistent with it.

There is a feeling abroad among contemporary Christians that the early Councils of the Church are a huge white elephant with which one is lumbered if one is a Roman Catholic, or Eastern Orthodox, or classical Protestant; and with which one may gratefully dispense if one is a liberal Protestant or existentialist Christian. It may be instructive at least to entertain an alternative possibility, that the decisions of the Councils can actually be of assistance to us in our own time to relate ourselves adequately to the wonderful mystery revealed in the New Testament. It has sometimes been suggested that, while the Fathers saved the faith for the Church, they used very inadequate conceptual tools in doing so. I have tried to show how sophisticated their tools in fact were, and how, on a number of points in theology and indeed in logic, contemporary scholars may have a thing or two to learn from them. Of course, there were and are many further refinements to be added, even if it be conceded that what was determined by the Councils ought to be retained. But it will not do to purport to improve on the Fathers' work without taking the measure of their real achievement. I have also tried to bring out how the formulae which at length were hammered out were not primarily the results of metaphysical speculation, but answers to questions which naturally and inevitably arise when one tries to make sense of the message of the New Testament as a whole.

Notes

1   R. P. C. Hanson in *The Times* (11 May 1974); quoted by A. Hardy, *The Biology of God* (London, 1975), p. 213. For a lively, and often acrimonious, discussion between philosophers and New Testament critics, on the actual or alleged results of New Testament criticism and their bearing on Christian faith, see *Hermes and Athena: Biblical*

Exegesis and Philosophical Theology, ed. Eleonore Stump and Thomas P. Flint (Notre Dame, 1993).

2 John Hick writes '... In all probability the historical Jesus ... neither thought of himself nor was thought of by his disciples as God incarnate': *God and the Universe of Faiths* (London, 1973), pp. 176–7. It is certain that he did not think or speak of his relation to God the Father in just these terms; they would not have been available to a man of his time and cultural situation. The important question is, however, whether he conceived and spoke of his relation with God the Father in a manner which was accurately expressed, in the context of a later culture and after a number of inevitable questions had arisen, in terms of the doctrine that he was God incarnate.

3 For a succinct evaluation of form-criticism from this point of view, see H. Riesenfeld, *The Gospel Tradition* (Oxford, 1970), pp. 5–6.

4 I have written at length on Bultmann elsewhere, and do not intend to repeat myself here (*Sense, Nonsense and Christianity* (London, 1964), pp. 250–70). In general, à propos of Bultmann's and similar positions, it should be pointed out that the absolutely justified principle, that Christian faith must not be allowed to dictate the results of historical investigation, twists easily into the quite different, and in my view definitely false, assumption, that no conceivable result of historical criticism would make any difference to essential Christian faith. I think that two impressive books on the problem of faith and history, Gerald Downing, *The Church and Jesus* (London, 1968) and Van Harvey, *The Historian and the Believer* (London, 1967), suffer from a failure to make the distinction clearly enough.

5 E. C. Hoskyns and N. Davey, *The Riddle of the New Testament* (London, 1931). Riesenfeld (op. cit., p. 149) commends this book, and reaffirms its general conclusions as regards the first three gospels, though he has a less historically sceptical attitude to the fourth.

6 Matthew 11:2–6; Luke 7:19–23.

7 Mark 4:41; Psalm 89:9.

8 Hoskyns and Davey, op. cit., pp. 173–4.

9 Mark 11:12–13; Matthew 21:18–19.

10 Luke 13:6–9.
11 Hoskyns and Davey, op. cit., pp. 174–5.
12 The classical expression of this view is A. Jülicher, *The Parables of Jesus* (Freiburg, 1888), p. 99. Jülicher was reacting, very justly, against the allegorical excesses of many earlier interpreters.
13 Mark 4:16–32.
14 Matthew 13:24–30.
15 Hosea 2:21–23.
16 Jeremiah 31:27–28; Isaiah 32:13–20.
17 Jeremiah 51:33; Joel 3:13; Hosea 6:11.
18 Psalm 126. The same ambiguous symbolism is marvellously exploited by William Blake in the Ninth Night of *The Four Zoas*.
19 Matthew 22:1–14; 25:1–13; Exodus 16:13–36.
20 Hoskyns and Davey, op. cit., pp. 184–8.
21 Riesenfeld, op. cit.
22 Hoskyns and Davey, op. cit., p. 14.
23 Ibid., pp. 162–3.
24 Ibid., pp. 282, 239–40.
25 See Sydney Temple, *The Core of the Fourth Gospel* (London and Oxford, 1975), pp. 3–7. An exhaustive survey of previous Johannine scholarship is to be had in R. Kysar, *The Fourth Evangelist and His Gospel* (Minneapolis, 1975). For a sceptical view of alleged 'development' in the understanding of Jesus by New Testament authors, and theories of literary dependence supporting and supported by this, see E. E. Ellis, 'Dating the New Testament', *New Testament Studies* (July 1980), pp. 487–502.
26 The pioneer here was P. Gardner-Smith, *Saint John and the Synoptic Gospels* (Cambridge, 1938). See also J. A. T. Robinson, *The Priority of John* (London, 1985).
27 Ibid., passim.
28 For detailed analysis of examples which show the difficulties in the supposition that John is in some way dependent on the synoptics, see Leon Morris, *Studies in the Fourth Gospel* (Grand Rapids, 1969), pp. 30–7.
29 Temple, op. cit., pp. 15–16, 9. Cf. C. H. Dodd, *Historical Tradition in the Fourth Gospel* (Cambridge, 1963), p. 427. Similar points are made by Raymond Brown in *New Testament Essays* (Milwaukee, 1965).

30 Temple, op. cit., pp. 22–3.
31 Ibid., p. 24.
32 C. H. Dodd, *The Interpretation of the Fourth Gospel* (Cambridge, 1953), p. 466; Morris, op. cit., p. 42.
33 Matthew 11:27; Luke 10:22.
34 John 12:24; 3:8. Dodd, *Historical Tradition in the Fourth Gospel*, pp. 115, 321, 419–20, 428.
35 Riesenfeld, op. cit., pp. 161–9.
36 Morris, op. cit., pp. 57–8; citing F. N. Davey in E. C. Hoskyns and N. Davey, *The Fourth Gospel* (London, 1947), p. 76.
37 O. Cullmann, *The Johannine Circle* (London, 1976), pp. 73–4, 25, 56.
38 Ibid., pp. 50–2, 90–1. On the thesis that the fourth gospel originated in the circle of Stephen and Philip, see B. Olsson, *Structure and Meaning in the Fourth Gospel* (Lund, 1974), p. 278.
39 Ibid., p. 89.
40 J. A. T. Robinson, *The Priority of John* (London, 1986).
41 J. Finegan, author of *The Archaeology of the New Testament* (Princeton, 1969); cited by Robinson, op. cit., p. 156.
42 Robinson, op. cit., p. 315. He cites John Marsh, *The Gospel of John* (Baltimore, 1968), p. 75.
43 Robinson, op. cit., pp. 316–17.
44 Ibid., pp. 318–19.
45 Ibid., pp. 306–7; citing A. M. Hunter, *According to John* (London and Philadelphia, 1968).
46 Robinson, op. cit., p. 30; citing M. Black, *An Aramaic Approach to the Gospels and Acts* (Oxford, 1971), p. 151.
47 Robinson, op. cit., p. 313; citing *Jesus and the Historian*, ed. F. C. Trotter (Philadelphia, 1968), p. 76.
48 Robinson, op. cit., p. 355.
49 Robinson, op. cit., p. 340.
50 Robinson, op. cit., pp. 125, 155–6. For the application of the principle to the production of a detailed chronology of the ministry of Jesus, see chapter 3. The claim of the fourth gospel to be based on eyewitness testimony finds unexpected support in the otherwise sceptical Robin Lane Fox: *The Unauthorized Version: Truth and Fiction in the Bible* (New York, 1991). This support is all the more striking, in that Fox is very hard on St Luke as a historian. John

Ashton's *Understanding the Fourth Gospel* (Oxford, 1991), which is in general a very impressive and enormously learned work, seems to me to throw very little light on the problem with which we are immediately concerned. Its comparison of the fourth gospel to a great work of art, while very just in itself, obscures rather than clarifies the fundamental dilemma which underlies 'the Johannine question': that the main authority behind this gospel is either a credible witness to the matters that he seems to report, or the most influential liar in history.

51 That there was a final editing by a member of the writer's school, who appears to have added chapter 21, is to be inferred from the work just as it stands (cf. John 19:35; 21:24).

52 See George Kennedy, 'Classical and Christian source criticism' in *The Relationships Among the Gospels: An Interdisciplinary Dialogue*, ed. William O. Walker (San Antonio, TX, 1978).

53 Pierson Parker, 'Two editions of John', *Journal of Biblical Literature* (1956), p. 304.

54 Temple, op. cit., p. 25. Cf. C. K. Barrett, *The Gospel According to St John* (London, 1978); also Ashton, op. cit. Much of Morris's book consists in an attempt to rebut in detail arguments by Barrett against the historicity of the gospel of John.

55 Temple, op. cit., p. 27.

56 Cf. Riesenfeld, op. cit., p. 28: 'In modern handbooks on the theology of the New Testament the appearance and proclamation of Jesus are sometimes treated as prolegomena. So regarded, Jesus of Nazareth belongs to the history of later Judaism. Christianity—that is, faith in Jesus as Messiah and redeemer—first arose in the primitive community after the resurrection and hence is to be treated as a subject separate from the preaching of Jesus. Over against this view, the considerations which have just been urged lead us back to the "classical" method of interpretation. The belief in Christ is to be found already in the words and deeds of Jesus just because Jesus regarded himself as the Messiah. The faith of the primitive Church had its origin in what Jesus proclaimed and set forth in symbolic form.'

57 B. Lonergan, *De Verbo Incarnato* (Rome, 1964), p. 22.
58 This is especially stressed by proponents of the so-called 'New Quest of the historical Jesus'. Cf. W. Pannenberg, *Jesus, God and Man* (London, 1968), pp. 53–66.
59 For collation of the texts in the New Testament which bear on the divinity of Christ, see Lonergan, *De Deo Trino I: Pars Dogmatica*, pp. 125–7 (Rome, 1964); *De Verbo Incarnato*, pp. 43–5, 61, 83–4, 93, 97.
60 2 Peter 1:1, Titus 2:13, Hebrews 1:9, John 20:28, 1 John 5:20.
61 For expression of this bewilderment by a famous theologian, cf. Hans Küng, *On Being a Christian* (London, 1977), p. 131: 'What is a Jew, a Chinese, a Japanese or an African, or even the average European or American today, to make of these Greek ciphers?'
62 B. Lonergan, *A Second Collection* (London, 1974), p. 23. I ought to add that the argument of the whole present section owes a great deal to Lonergan.
63 On methods proposed for resolving this paradox, see Chapter 5 below.
64 Mark 2:22.
65 Father Sergius Bulgakov, the Russian Orthodox theologian, puts it: 'The Holy Bible . . . is not concerned with systematic theology. It presents us with its similitudes in the form of theological raw material, so to speak. It is the task of biblical theology to understand and to compare these similitudes': *The Wisdom of God* (London, 1937), p. 34.
66 Lonergan, *Second Collection*, op. cit., pp. 25–6.
67 Nestorius was right to protest that he was not a 'Nestorian', in the sense of holding that Jesus and the eternal Word were two persons. However, in denying that Mary was mother of God, as Cyril acutely observed, he was logically committed to Nestorianism. If Mary is mother of Jesus, but not mother of God, then Jesus cannot be God.
68 For example, Boethius, Richard of St Victor, and Thomas Aquinas.
69 For suggestions on this matter, see Chapter 5 below.
70 Cf. L. Dewart, *The Future of Belief* (New York, 1966), p. 150.

71 E.g., A. T. Hanson. Similar difficulties have been raised by
    Piet Schoonenberg in *The Christ* (New York, 1971).
72 A. T. Hanson, *Grace and Truth* (London, 1975), p. 1. Cf.
    Lonergan, *Second Collection*, op. cit., pp. 254f.

F I V E

Consciousness and the Trinity

'Very well, let us concede for the sake of argument, that the doctrine of the atonement is not morally repulsive, and that the doctrine of the incarnation is not historically indefensible. Does it not still remain that the doctrine of the Trinity, which has usually been supposed to be central to Christianity, is an insoluble contradiction, and a pointless contradiction at that? Really it is not surprising that so many theologians who would call themselves Christians are now at last abandoning it.'

It is obvious that the doctrine of the Trinity does, at first sight, appear to be a contradiction, since God is represented by it, to put the matter crudely, both as three entities and as one entity.[1] But before one concludes that it is a contradiction, and so ought to be rejected without more ado, it seems worth attending to the attempts which have been made by serious Christian thinkers to cope with this problem. A number of theologians have suggested that it is human consciousness which can provide us with an analogy by which we can achieve some understanding, however imperfect, of the mystery of the Trinity. The view seems hinted at in John's gospel and first epistle, was explicitly set out by Augustine, and was worked out in detail by Thomas Aquinas. What seems to be the essence of this comparison of human consciousness to the Trinity is this. God is eternal and unrestricted understanding and love; while human beings develop little by little in understanding of themselves and one another, and in both respects are liable to corruption and regression as well as to authentic development. The doctrine of the Trinity, in its characteristically Western form,[2] is to the effect that God as Father 'begets' God as Son, and that God as Holy Spirit 'proceeds from' both. Interpreted in terms of the psychological analogy, this is to say that infinite understanding forms a conception of itself, and infinite love is evinced in accordance with this conception. As forming this conception God is Father, as the conception so formed God is Son, and as the love evinced in accordance with this conception God is Holy Spirit. In this understanding, conceiving and loving of self, God understands, conceives and loves all else that exists; to be asked to share in the divine life, as Christians believe humankind has been, is to be invited to an unimaginable increase in that understanding and loving which are themselves nothing but a creaturely image of God.[3]

Given that there is an analogy of the kind suggested between the Holy Trinity and human consciousness, it may be asked what practical or pastoral significance, if any, there is in the comparison. The clue is to be found in the doctrine that humanity is created in the image of God, and its corollary that it is the paramount duty and interest of human beings to preserve and foster the reflection within themselves of God who is true conception *because of* unrestricted understanding, and infinite love *because of* unrestricted understanding and true conception. Humanity's prime sin, and the source of all its other sins, is that distortion and inversion of the divine image which consists of the mutual reinforcement of ignorance and misplaced affection. This is the road to hell, which is the absence of God. For the more we distort the divine image in us, the more motives we have for avoiding God; since to come closer to God is to come closer to the truth about ourselves, and the more we have protected our self-esteem with self-deception the more painful this is.

What is it to have an understanding of oneself, to form a conception and evince approval accordingly? An example lies to hand in one of P. G. Wodehouse's school stories. A boy called Mike Jackson has just succeeded, much to his own surprise, in beating another boy called Adair in a fight. This leads him to form a new conception of himself, and rather to approve of himself as so conceived.

> *The feat [of beating Adair] presented that interesting person, Mike Jackson, to him in a fresh and pleasing light, as one who had had a tough job to face and had carried it through. Jackson, the cricketer, he knew, but Jackson, the deliverer of knock-out blows, was strange to him, and he found this new acquaintance a man to be respected.*[4]

Someone might say—and indeed Karl Barth has said[5]—that the notion of 'person' as used in the doctrine of the Trinity is quite distinct from that of a human person. Now for Augustine, the word 'person' in this context was certainly nothing more than a convenient label for whatever it was that there are three of in the Trinity.[6] Later theologians tried to specify the matter further. According to a formula which expresses Thomas Aquinas's view,[7] a person is 'a distinct subsistent in an intellectual nature', which does seem to entail that the 'persons' of the Trinity are persons in something like the same sense that human individuals are so. You and I are 'distinct' from one another, and are of 'an intellectual nature' in that we understand, we will one state of affairs as opposed to another, and so on. And one may infer from what is said about God the Father, Christ and (more controversially[8]) the Holy Spirit in the New Testament, that they are distinct both from one another and from us, and 'personal' in the senses that I have just mentioned. But preoccupation with persons or conscious subjects as such—with what they are, how they develop, what goes wrong with them in the course of development, how this can be put right, how they are related to one another within communities, and how this affects them for better or for worse—is comparatively modern. If one is to do theology properly in a contemporary milieu, one has to attend to the question of what bearing such inquiries have on one's understanding of the doctrine of the Trinity. Otherwise the doctrine, so far as it is retained at all by contemporary Christians, will inevitably seem more and more a mere embarrassment to them—a sort of dogmatic white elephant which has been inherited more or less reluctantly from a less enlightened past.

As human persons, we largely exist, and are what we are, in and through our relations with other persons. It may seem odd to cite medieval Councils of the Church on such a matter; but perhaps every now and then one may learn a thing or two from them. According to the Council of Florence, what I have just said is partly true of us is wholly true of the divine persons, who are distinct only in and through their mutual relations;[9] the Father *as begetting* the Son; the Son *as begotten by* the Father; the Holy Spirit *as proceeding from* Father and Son.

It may be asked what biblical foundation there is, if any, for the use of such a psychological analogy for our understanding of the Trinity. The First Epistle of John says that God is light and love;[10] and for 'light' one may well, in accordance with a common symbolism, read knowledge or understanding. The Gospel of John speaks of an eternal Word who was with God, and of a Spirit who comes both from God and from God's Son who is the Word.[11] In addition, it claims that to love and to hold to the truth is to share the life of God the Father, the Son, and the Spirit; whereas lies, malice and even murder are characteristic of the refusal and repudiation of this life.[12] One may conclude, I think, that the analogy is not entirely without biblical foundation.

Human consciousness, in its usual rather corrupt form, seems basically to be a kind of inverted image of the Trinity as conceived in accordance with the psychological analogy. It is characteristic of the person with corrupt consciousness that he cannot 'face' himself; that is to say, because he hates himself as he would conceive himself if he proceeded honestly in accordance with the available evidence, he has to abuse understanding in order to form a conception of himself sufficiently gratifying to his self-esteem. If in God perfect love is evinced in accordance with a conception which is framed on the basis of un-restricted understanding, in human beings it is always to a considerable extent the case that distorted affection and avoidance of understanding reinforce one another. If I have a clear conception of the effect I have on others, and of how others see me in consequence of this, it is liable to deliver a vicious blow to my self-esteem. Thus it is usually rather more pleasant, and much less morally and intellectually exacting, either to form a false conception of their attitude towards me, or to affect hatred and con-tempt towards them for their actual attitude, or to settle (as most of us do most of the time) for some compromise between these two.[13] What applies to relations between individuals, again, applies to relations between groups. The self-esteem of each group is buttressed by 'social lies', as Berdyaev called them, which its members share about rival groups. In speaking of religion, Freud said that, by sharing in the universal neurosis, the individual spares himself the trouble of constructing his own individual neurosis.[14] But the group rivalries which I have mentioned are at least as characteristically social, professional or (low be it spoken) political as religious in nature.

The breaking-up of the systems of illusion which we build to protect ourselves is a very painful business. There are some fine passages describing the destruction of a small-scale system, in the case of a person already endowed with a more than average share of self-know-ledge, in Jane Austen's *Pride and Prejudice*. Of Darcy, Elizabeth Bennet says: 'I meant to be uncommonly clever in taking so decided a dislike to him, without any reason. It is such a spur to one's genius, such an opening for wit, to have a dislike of that kind.'[15] Of her disillusionment about Wickham, she says: 'How humiliating is this discovery! Yet, how just a humiliation! Had I been in love, I could not have been more wretchedly blind! Yet vanity, not love has been my folly. Pleased with the preference of one [Wickham], and offended by the neglect of the other [Darcy], on the very beginning of our acquaintance, I have courted prepossession and ignorance, and driven reason away where either was concerned. Till this moment, I never knew myself.'[16] These passages bring out with extraordinary clarity what it is for a person to move from a comparatively distorted to a comparatively just conception both of herself and of what the psychiatrists would call 'significant others', and to redirect her feelings and attitudes accordingly.

It is perhaps obvious, when one comes to think of it, that our development towards moral and spiritual maturity is a matter of our reaction to situations which, like that described by Jane Austen, confront us with the alternative: either to attend to the evidence in hand, form a fresh conception of ourselves and others in deference to it, and make our evaluations and decisions accordingly; or to shirk the moral shock of self-recognition, brush the relevant evidence aside, and either physically avoid, or exert moral pressure on, those persons who might obtrude on our attention an inconvenient amount of the truth. Since it is a very painful business, both for personal and for social reasons, to break vicious circles of intellectual and moral corruption, it is no wonder that most of us usually avoid doing so.

One of the most useful devices for such avoidance is that of 'projection', in which, as Thomas Love Peacock expresses it, I lay on external things the blame for my mind's internal disorder.[17] It's not my pathological irritableness, it's just that I meet so many stupid people; it's not my bad teaching, it's the lousy students one gets these days; and so on and so on. Though the unmasking of oneself by oneself is in the long run the only way either to social health or to harmony between people, it is to be emphasized how difficult and often dangerous this is. A group of psychiatrists once invented a handy technique for showing people to themselves. While most of their patients suffered a moral shock which was followed by a marked improvement in their condition, one closed himself in his garage and switched on the engine of his car. As Jung says, the illusions would not be so prevalent if they did not serve some useful purpose.[18] Anyone who strives for self-knowledge and the withdrawal of projections soon finds that this is the way of the cross.[19] 'Everyone carries a shadow', he writes, 'and the less it is embodied in the individual's conscious life, the blacker and denser it is.'[20] What makes it worse is that we project our shadow onto others; it is *they* who are wrong, who must be fought or treated with contempt. Anyone brave enough to withdraw these projections is conscious of a considerable shadow of her own, and knows that much of the evil in the world is latent, or not so latent, in herself. She 'has succeeded in shouldering at least an infinitesimal part of the gigantic unsolved problems of our day. These problems are mostly so difficult because they are poisoned by mutual projections.'[21]

For Jean-Paul Sartre, especially in his early period, the real 'I' is exactly what I do not share, what I keep to myself. If someone else really knows what I am up to, to that extent she destroys me as a person. This is the point of his famous example of the man peering through a keyhole into a hotel room, who suddenly realizes that someone else is looking at him doing this.[22] It follows, of course, first, that God does not exist; since God's omniscience would destroy us all—if God existed, God would *always* be looking at *every* person who was up to something he wanted to keep to himself. Second, it follows that love is impossible. Since no one can possibly know me thoroughly and accept me as I am, a close human relationship is bound to be one of conflict; if it is not that of sadism and masochism, where one party delights to destroy, the other to be immolated. Fortunately for us all, most lovers, close friends, and parents and children, know by experience that Sartre is wrong; that however brilliantly he analyses the pathology of human relationships, he ignores the most important possibility that lies within them. The best of sexual love, or of any kind of friendship, is that each subject is both known thoroughly and accepted as she is by the other; and is in a way within her, as Aquinas says, as known in knower and beloved in lover.[23] This is supremely so in the case of the triune God, who is the perfect example at once of self-knowledge and properly-ordered self-love, and of mutual knowledge and mutual love. All creatures are fully known and loved by God; it is the privilege of theists, and especially of Christians, that the knowledge and love is mutual, that they consciously share in the life of God and hope for a consummation of that sharing in future.[24]

Solzhenitsyn's *The Gulag Archipelago* is a regular anthology of examples of group self-deception and its effects. On one occasion, the Soviet government under Stalin had set the country's engineers an impossible task; but rather than admit that they had made a stupid and costly mistake, it was decided to allege incompetence or malice on the part of the engineers, and to deflect the just indignation of the public accordingly.

> *For the engineers (those who were free, not yet imprisoned, and who had to face the necessity of working cheerfully after the defamation at the trial of their whole class) there was no way out. They were damned if they did and damned if they didn't. If they went forward, it was wrong, and if they went backward, it was wrong too. If they hurried, it was hurrying for the purpose of wrecking. If they moved methodically, it meant*

> *wrecking by slowing down tempos. If they were*
> *painstaking in developing some branch of industry, it*
> *was intended delay, sabotage. And if they indulged in*
> *capricious leaps, their intention was to produce an*
> *imbalance for the purpose of wrecking. Using capital for*
> *repairs, improvements, or capital readiness was tying*
> *up capital funds. And if they allowed equipment to be*
> *used until it broke down, it was a diversionary action.*[25]

When institutions claim in effect to represent the ideal, like Communist governments, or Catholic and to some extent other Christian churches, the motives of this kind of self-deception are particularly strong. In such cases, any admission of fundamental theoretical error or moral fault, let alone of both in combination, may seem to threaten the collapse of a whole way of life and system of values.

One should certainly not underestimate the difficulty involved, or allow the atrocious harm that they do to induce one to withhold sympathy from those unable or unwilling to face it. It is not easy, for example, for the accredited leaders of the proletariat to admit that they have concealed their own incompetence and irresponsibility by making the same kind of unjust and hypocritical charges for which they rightly condemn bourgeois governments; or that they have covered up the fact of the impossibility of their programmes by punishing on plausible pretexts those involved in the inevitable failure to carry them out. When you have absolute control of the press and of broadcasting, and thus can quash any adverse publicity put about by other people, do you not have almost to be a saint publicly to admit your guilt? And, of course, the business of lying and persecuting is cumulative, assuming that your control of information and of people's response to it is less than absolute; you have to lie and persecute in order to conceal the fact that you are lying and persecuting. And the greater your deception of yourself and others, and the more elaborate the system of oppression and mystification that you have constructed to defend it, the more motive you have for avoiding enlightenment. The darkening of the image of the Trinity in human beings is a cumulative and self-reinforcing process.

Some kinds of group self-deception are due not so much to any specific motive, as to what Durkheim called the 'moral mediocrity' of ordinary life—the lack of heroic feats to be performed and deadly dangers to be undergone in the ordinary course of bourgeois existence. To get over this, there is nothing like indulgence of inter-group hatred, which is always helped on by judicious misrepresentation. This reinforcement of hatred by misrepresentation is, as I have already suggested, of the essence of the distortion of the divine image in human beings.

How on earth is the process to be reversed, when to maintain and elaborate the network of malice and illusion is so much more convenient on the whole for every individual and every dominant group? Intellectual arguments carry little or no weight, as the Marxists have noted, with those in the grip of ideology. It is thus no wonder that they have concluded that the only solution is to tear down the economic and social structures which give rise to all the deception and misrepresentation, and even to the existence of people who, as Marx and Engels put it, 'make the perfecting of the illusion of the class about itself their chief source of livelihood'.[26] But one might perhaps wonder, in the light of what has actually happened, whether the successful revolutionary class will be liable to be much freer of illusions than the class which it has supplanted.

In a passage from his *Introductory Lectures on Psycho-analysis*, Freud speaks of the need for some emotional *rapport* between patient and analyst if the patient is to be brought to acknowledge the truth about herself. Without love and trust on the patient's part

The physician and his arguments would never even be

107

listened to. Faith . . . is a derivative of love and at first it
needed no arguments. Not until later does it admit them
so far as to take them into critical consideration if they
have been offered by someone who is loved. Without this
support arguments have no weight with the patient, never
do have any with most people in life.[27]

The parallel with religious love of God, and the resultant
trust in God which (at least ideally) enables a person to
face the truth about herself, is obvious enough. At least
unless we have that 'basic trust'[28] which is the precon-
dition for the good will and the resolution to deal with
our illusions, mental ingenuity will be worse than useless,
as we will employ it merely to weave a more elaborate
tangle of rationalizations. That God has, in the incarnation, made a special gesture to invite and inspire such
human love is, of course, the special claim of Christians.

Marx claimed that one had to stand Hegel on his head
in order to get at the truth. I have tried to illustrate how
the truth about the corrupt human consciousness is to be
had by standing on its head the doctrine of the Trinity as
explicated in terms of the psychological analogy. This
explication helps at once to make some sense of the doctrine, and to bring out its relevance for human living. We
are faithful images of the Trinity so far as we increase in
just conception and honourable love of ourselves and of
one another;[29] we corrupt the divine image so far as we
darken understanding and distort conception in the
interests of hatred, and foster hatred in deference to mis-
understanding and misconception.

Notes

1   Those Christians who are inclined to appeal to the
propriety of 'paradoxical' discourse in theology at this
point might do well to consider the caustic dictum of

C. Hartshorne: 'A theological paradox, it appears, is what a contradiction becomes when it is about God rather than something else, or indulged in by a theologian or a church rather than an unbeliever or heretic.' He adds: 'If paradoxes are not accepted as signs that we are thinking badly, what signs would we recognize?': *The Divine Relativity* (New Haven, 1948), pp. 1–4.

2 Eastern Christendom does not recognize the Spirit as proceeding *from the Son* as well as from the Father.

3 See Augustine, *De Trinitate* XV, xii, 22; Aquinas, *Summa Theologica* I, xxvii, a. 1 c.; a. 3 ad 3m; a. 1 ad 2m; B. Lonergan, *Verbum: Word and Idea in Aquinas* (London, 1968), Introduction and chapter V; *De Deo Trino*, II: *Pars Systematica* (Rome, 1964), p. 70. It will be obvious that this chapter owes a great deal to Lonergan.

4 P. G. Wodehouse, *The World of Psmith* (London, 1974), p. 113.

5 Karl Barth, *Church Dogmatics* (Edinburgh, 1936), I, 1, p. 403.

6 Augustine, *De Trinitate* V, ix, 10.

7 Aquinas does not use exactly this formula himself; but it has been taken, rightly so far as I can judge, to convey the essentials of his position.

8 One might say that the following texts from the New Testament, taken together, are an adequate foundation for the conviction that the Holy Spirit is both a real person and distinct from both the Father and the Son: Matthew 10:20; John 14:26; 15:26; 16:7, 13; Acts 8:29, 39; 10:19; 11:12; 16:6, 7; Romans 8:26; 1 Corinthians 12:11, 12; Ephesians 4:30.

9 H. Denzinger, *Enchiridion Symbolorum*, ed. K. Rahner (Freiburg, 1960), p. 703.

10 1 John 1:5; 4:8, 16.

11 John 1:1, 2; 16:13–15.

12 John 1:10; 5:24; 13:34–35; 14:15–17, 21, 23; 15:21; 16:2–3; 17:25.

13 The works of R. D. Laing abound in instructive examples.

14 S. Freud, *The Future of an Illusion* (London, 1928), p. 77.

15 Jane Austen, *Pride and Prejudice* (London, 1882 edn), II, p. 7.

16 Ibid., II, p. 3.

17 Thomas Love Peacock, *Nightmare Abbey* (London, 1924 edn), p. 2.

18 C. G. Jung, *Mysterium Coniunctionis (Collected Works*, vol. XIV; London, 1963), p. 520.

19 Jung, *Psychology and Religion (Collected Works*, vol. XI, London, 1958), p. 179.

20 Jung, *Mysterium Coniunctionis*, p. 76.

21 Jung, *Psychology and Religion*, p. 82.

22 J. P. Sartre, *Being and Nothingness* (London, 1957), pp. 259ff.

23 Aquinas, *Summa Theologica* I, xxxiv, a. 33; xxxvii, a. 2. Cf. Lonergan, *De Deo Trino*, II, pp. 250–3.

24 This is not inconsistent with God's giving the gift of God's love in and through other religious traditions. But if the Spirit who is God's love is the Spirit of the Son, and the Son is made man, those who receive the Spirit explicitly through the Son made man do have a special privilege. Cf. Lonergan, *A Second Collection* (London, 1974), pp. 174–5; *Philosophy of God and Theology* (London, 1973), p. 67.

25 A. Solzhenitsyn, *The Gulag Archipelago* (London, 1974), p. 283.

26 In *The German Ideology*. See D. McLellan, *The Thought of Karl Marx: An Introduction* (London, 1971), p. 154.

27 S. Freud, *Introductory Lectures on Psychoanalysis* (London, 1933), pp. 372–3.

28 E. H. Erikson in particular has emphasized the central place of basic trust in psychic life. See 'Growth and crises of the healthy personality' in *Personality*, ed. R. S. Lazarus and E. M. Opton (Harmondsworth, 1970), pp. 169–70, 179–80. For the bearing of basic trust on morality and religion, see D. Evans, *Struggle and Fulfilment: The Inner Dynamics of Religion and Morality* (Toronto, 1979).

29 A properly-ordered self-love, as Augustine noted, is presupposed in the command to love our neighbours as ourselves. Cf. E. Gilson, *The Christian Philosophy of St Augustine* (London, 1961), pp. 166–7.

SIX

Life after death

'Very well then', our sceptic might say, 'let us grant, for the sake of argument, that you have made some sense of the doctrines of the incarnation and the Trinity. There is still one overwhelming objection to Christianity, as indeed to all forms of traditional religious belief. The religions are committed ineluctably to belief in some kind of future life. Such a belief was relatively plausible in past times, when it seemed natural to parcel human beings out into the "soul", the inner private, thinking and feeling part on the one hand; and the "body", the public part perceivable to the senses, on the other. But the whole of contemporary science and philosophy converges on the view that we are, when all is said and done, nothing but elaborately organized parcels of matter. The expectation of life after death is a relic of a superstitious past, and has no more solid basis than a mixture of pride and wish-fulfilment. Thought and feeling, even if they are not just the same as states of the brain, are absolutely dependent on them.

'Not only is any kind of expectation of life after death, whether as a surviving soul, as a living body resurrected at the end of time, or in some reincarnate form, incredible as a matter of fact; but, as recent philosophers have taught us, it is very doubtful if it even makes sense. Suppose someone who looks like John Smith, and has vivid impressions which are just like memories of having been John Smith, is brought into existence a thousand years or more after that individual's death. In what sense could the person be anything but a good copy of John Smith? It is all very well talking about continuity of memory; but memory presupposes personal identity, and so identity of body; and consequently cannot be used to establish it. As for "disembodied persons", we acquire our concept of a person by interacting with beings of flesh and blood. To take away the body is to take away the person. Death is not lived through, and if it were, it would not be death. The conception of reincarnation is objectionable for just the same reason as that of a resurrected body or reconstituted person.'[1]

It appears to me that there are three kinds of reasons that someone might give for believing in life after death; which may roughly be described as religious, philosophical, and empirical. I will briefly summarize these, and give an estimate of what weight should be given to each kind of consideration. Finally I will comment on the philosophical objections that I have just mentioned.

The religious reasons might be set out as follows. There are grounds for belief that there is a God, and that God has revealed the divine nature and purposes for humankind rather in the manner that I have argued so far in this book. That there is life after death for human beings, either as disembodied spirits or as resurrected bodily persons or both, is part and parcel of this revelation. It may also be remarked, that it is a necessary consequence of the belief that the Creator is just; since there is hardly any proposition more certain, than that the good are not always rewarded, and the wicked are not always punished, when only the present life is taken into account. Now, whatever the merits of this view of the matter, it is notable that most Christian theologians and apologists of the past have not contented themselves with it; they have tried to supply other reasons for believing in life after death. And the philosophical arguments which I have advanced might make it appear that, if any system of doctrine has the logical consequence that there is life after death for human beings, then that system of doctrine is thereby shown to be false. If something cannot possibly be true, then whatever implies it cannot possibly be true either.

In the past, many philosophers argued that human beings are not in fact reducible without remainder to their bodily aspects; and therefore that it is possible that the aspect of us which is other than bodily might survive the dissolution of our bodies. In fact there have been two standard views within Christian thought of the relation between the 'soul' and the 'body'. The first, which is due especially to Plato, and was expounded notoriously by René Descartes, is that of extreme dualism. The human being on this view, as Augustine put it, is an immortal soul using a mortal and perishable body.[2] Essentially the soul is that part of us which thinks and wills, as opposed to being of a certain chemical composition and anatomical arrangement; on what side the sensing and feeling aspect of us lies is a matter of dispute. (Some would say that, as items of direct consciousness, they form a part of the soul; others that their dependence on the body is evident in a way that that of other aspects of consciousness is not.) On this account the immortality of the soul follows more or less as a matter of course; the soul is freed from the body to which it has no essential relationship, and with which it is temporarily encumbered. However, the doctrine of the resurrection of the body, which has always repre-sented the primary focus of Christian hope, is by no means so satisfactorily accounted for on this view. Would it not be a punishment rather than a reward, if God reunited us with bodies from which the whole moral purpose of life was to release us? Just the opposite applies to the other view, which is exemplified most notably by Aristotle's psychology; soul is related to a body as form to matter, as the table is related to the wood, the goblet to the glass, or the statue to the marble out of which it

113

is made. To suppose that the 'soul' might survive the dissolution of the 'body', on this account, may well seem as nonsensical as to suppose that the essential goblet could go on existing after the shattering of the glass out of which it was made.

In support of mildly or radically dualist views, one may point out the curious relationship of consciousness and thought to the material world. In a book about Freud and his followers, J. A. C. Brown refers to a series of important developments in modern thought, all of which represent blows to human pride. Up to the end of medieval times, he says, human beings assumed that the earth which they inhabited was at the very centre of things. But then Copernicus showed that the earth was by no means at the centre of the universe; and we now know that even the sun is only a comparatively tiny object in the outskirts of a galaxy consisting of billions of stars, which is itself merely one of billions of galaxies. Next, Darwin showed that human beings were nothing but highly evolved and differentiated animals. The final step was taken by Freud, who showed, so the author says, that the vaunted human mind is as much use for discovering truth as a pig's snout.[3] The author did not appear to realize that he had written anything very paradoxical; and yet one may wonder how on this view Freud himself, apart from divine inspiration perhaps, was able to find the truth on this or any other matter. If mind is really simply a function of the behaviour of very complicated organisms according to physical laws, which many people think is a necessary consequence of science, it is very difficult to account for science itself. Science after all depends on minds being sufficiently independent of physical laws to be able to attend to evidence, form hypotheses, and accept in each case the hypothesis which best accounts for the evidence. Unless we believed that scientists proceeded in this way, there would be no reason to take seriously what they said or wrote as telling us what is likely to be true about the world. It looks as though the 'mental' aspect of ourselves must at least to some degree be independent of the 'physical', for science itself to be possible. In general, we seem to have two radically different ways of explaining the things and events of our world, neither of which appears to be reducible to the other. Some things and states of affairs we regard as due to entirely physical causes and processes, such as sunsets, the growth of trees, radioactive decay, and so forth; while we attribute others to conscious agency, like speeches, pranks, books, revolutions, and wars. But if this aspect of human beings is thus in some degree independent of the material world and its physical laws, it may be asked, is it not at least conceivable that it might last beyond the dissolution of the aspect of ourselves which is thus dependent?[4]

To put what is nearly the same point in another way, it is a remarkable feature of our human world, though of course we take it for granted the whole time, that some things or events can be *about* other things or events, can signify or represent them. A sentence in a book can be about Eleanor of Aquitaine, a lecture by a professor of astronomy can be about quasars. (A thought or a statement may even be about something which does not exist, like a naturally-occurring trans-uranic element, or the highest prime number, or the present Queen of Mexico.) This relationship of 'aboutness' does seem, at least at first sight, to be ineluctably dependent on minds. If I leave a bit of bank paper on the floor of my office, and inadvertently tread on it while I am wearing muddy boots, it is conceivable that, by a strange coincidence, the result might be useful as a map for someone trying to find her way about the campus of the University of Calgary. But I do not think it would make sense to say that it *was* a map of that campus, until it had occurred to someone to use it as such. Materialists are apt to invoke computers at this point; here, surely, they say, we have material and mechanistic systems which are capable of meaning things and states of affairs. But the same surely applies to computers as to maps; their capacity to mean depends in the long run on the intentions of conscious beings other than themselves. The series of letters which sometimes appears on the screen of my wordprocessor, 'You may now switch off safely', only means that I may now switch off safely by virtue of the fact that it has been deliberately programmed by someone else to do so. 'Aboutness', one may conclude, may be either original or derived. Certainly, mere physical objects and states of affairs can be about other objects and states of affairs; but such 'aboutness' is always derived. Original 'aboutness', it seems, can only be characteristic of the conscious states of beings who have minds.

Even if the arguments which I have just outlined, about the irreducibility of the mental to the physical, are impossible to refute (and of course many would claim that in principle they can be refuted), they still do not establish that the 'soul' is liable to survive the death of the 'body'. Why can one not say that mind is an admittedly irreducible feature of some physical objects, which arises with a certain degree of complexity of physical organization and behaviour, and perishes with it? While it may perhaps make some sort of sense to suppose that the mental aspect of ourselves outlasts the physical, the overwhelming evidence, it might be insisted, is to the effect that as a matter of fact it does not. This seems to lead directly to the empirical question, of whether there may not be some evidence in experience which goes to confirm after all the view that the 'soul' or conscious personality somehow survives the death of the 'body'.

Stories about contacts by the living with the spirits of the dead have of course been told and retold among human beings of a vast range of cultures and backgrounds from time immemorial. But it was not until the late nineteenth century that attempts were made to apply the methods of science to these accounts. There had been a craze for 'spiritualism' since about the middle of the century; it became fashionable to hold sittings with 'mediums', who after going into trance appeared to transmit messages from the dead. Among the huge mass of sentimental trivia which emerged in this process, some material was impressive enough to convince a number of learned persons that here was something which at least was worthy of serious investigation. So there were founded, in the 1880s, the British and the American Societies for Psychical Research. One might have expected that, in course of the century which has elapsed since then, the learned world would have made up its mind one way or the other about the reality of the phenomena in question, or the bearing of these, if indeed they are real, on the question of life after death. But the melancholy fact is, that this is by no means the case. Many mediums, including those who have produced some of the most impressive results, have been detected in fraud. Of the two Fox sisters, who may be said to have inaugurated the spiritualist craze, one 'confessed' to fraud many years later; though her sister repudiated the allegation, and there have not been lacking suggestions that the 'confession' had other motives than the desire to tell the truth.

While the scientific community has in general been contemptuous of or actively hostile to these investigations, some first-rate scientists, including Alfred Russel Wallace, Sir William Crookes, and Sir Oliver Lodge, have become convinced as a result of them that the spirits of the dead survive, and sometimes communicate with human beings. But those who are seriously interested in these matters are still as divided as they were a century ago about whether the alleged phenomena actually occur, and whether, if they do, this constitutes evidence that the human personality is capable of surviving bodily death. The phenomena seem maddeningly elusive, and the path of the sincere investigator is crisscrossed with false trails of misinformation and outright imposture. And yet it may seem irrational to dismiss out of hand such a large range of alleged cases, when data often seem well-corroborated and the witnesses inimpeachable. As to the attitude of believing scientists, it is often pointed out by sceptics that

117

such persons, even when eminent in their fields, are not usually expert in conjuring, and so are incompetent to detect skilful cheating. However, there have been cases, like the sittings of Eusapia Palladino in Naples, where good conjurors have been convinced, against their will, that the phenomena which they appeared to be witnessing were genuine.

But it may properly be objected, that it is one thing to grant that such phenomena take place; another to conclude that the spirits of the dead are responsible for them. That such phenomena may well occur, but are always better explained in another way, has been argued in a classical article by E. R. Dodds.[5] Suppose one comes across an apparently impressive case, in which the spirit of a person recently dead appears to contact one of her relatives through a medium. A piece of information is given which at first sight no one but the dead person could have known, which later turns out to be true. Let us say that it is to the effect that a rare coin is to be found at the back of the third drawer, which is hardly ever opened, of the chest of drawers in the bedroom where the deceased person used to sleep. The search is duly made, and a rare coin is found. The bereaved person may well be impressed with such apparently strong evidence that the deceased not only goes on existing in a disembodied form, but has been able and willing to make contact with someone still living. However, the sceptic may point out that there are a number of other hypotheses which will account for the phenomenon. The medium may have been 'clairvoyant', and hence capable of knowing about the coin in the dresser by paranormal means. Or she may have employed telepathy to read the unconscious mind of the sitter, who herself had unconscious knowledge of the fact. It is liable to be objected, of course, that these are extravagant hypotheses. But who is to say that they are more extravagant than that of the survival by a human personality of bodily death, and the ability and willingness of that personality to communicate with the living? Dodds suggests that even the most impressive cases can be explained without resort to the hypothesis of survival; and therefore ought to be so explained.

In the last decade or so, as a result of improvements in medical care, there have been many more cases than before of persons who return to full consciousness after being clinically dead. Quite a high proportion of these report a selection from a definite range of experiences—of seeing their body from a point several feet away from it; of going through a tunnel; of moving towards or emerging into a light; of meeting dead friends and relatives; of encountering a 'being of light' who is impressive, sympathetic and knowledgeable; of coming against some kind of fence or barrier which they cannot pass; of being reluctant to return to their body; and so on.[6] Those who undergo these experiences very often have a changed attitude to life, and are apt to come to believe in life after death when they did not previously do so. But however subjectively impressive these experiences, and whatever their psychological effects on those who undergo them, it may still be doubted whether they have any real evidential value.[7] Given the structure of the human brain, one might expect it to produce rather similar hallucinations when a person is on the brink of death, whether she recovers or not. Does not such a feature as the tunnel leading towards light, moreover, look suspiciously like a reactivation of the universal experience of being born? And the probable effect of drugs administered to allay the patient's anxiety, or to dull her pain, must not be left out of account.

It has been objected that the fact that these patients recover strictly implies that they were never really dead at all; hence their testimony must be worthless on the subject of what happens to people or their 'souls' after death.[8] But I think that this objection neglects the important fact that, owing to the spectacular advances in modern medicine, death is no longer quite the all-or-nothing affair that it once seemed obviously to be. There are various medical criteria of death—including cessation of breathing, stopping of the heart, the end of electrical activity in the brain, and the irreversibility of these conditions. Would it not be rather misleading, if the first three of these criteria applied in some case, but not the fourth, to say roundly and unequivocally that the patient had not died, simply on the ground that she recovered? It appears to me that, in a case like the one I have just described, the question 'Did she die' could not properly be answered with a straight 'yes' or 'no'. One could only say something like 'Well, according to many of the usual criteria, she was dead; but she was not dead in the sense that her condition proved irreversible'. If the argument that I have just given is sound, I do not think that the relevance of near-death experiences to the question of survival can be dismissed out of hand. But the difficulties which I mentioned in the last paragraph and the one before it still remain.

Some have concluded that such considerations invalidate all the empirical evidence which apparently supports the hypothesis of life after death; it is often maintained, in fact, that psychical research has reached an impasse on the question. However, one can conceive of other ways of approach to it. In 1916, the English physicist Sir Oliver Lodge cited the French philosopher Henri Bergson as follows:

> *Professor Bergson . . . urged that statements about life on the other side, properly studied, . . . might ultimately furnish proof more logically cogent than was possible from mere access to earth-memories . . . I am inclined to think that the time is getting ripe now for the production and discussion of material of this technically unverifiable kind; to be scrutinized and tested by internal consistency and inherent probability, in the same sort of way as travellers' tales have to be scrutinized and tested.[9]*

I am not sure what 'inherent probability' would amount to in these matters; but the criterion of internal consistency, given that enough relevant material could be obtained, would seem to be a good deal more promising. For when a great many witnesses agree in their testimony, given that collusion between them is impossible or at best extremely unlikely, it becomes highly improbable that what they all say is false; even when it is granted that, if one takes each piece of evidence separately, it is virtually worthless. So far as I know, a moose has never been seen on the campus of the University of Calgary, though such an event is not in principle impossible. But suppose I find five persons, of whom three are drunk, and the other two notoriously unreliable, all claiming that a moose has been seen at that location. I surely ought to take their joint testimony seriously, at least so far as collusion between them has been ruled out as virtually impossible.

The suggestion of Bergson and Lodge was not taken up till several decades later, when a distinguished British geologist, Robert Crookall, decided to devote his retirement to doing so. He published the first results of his inquiries in 1961, in *The Supreme Adventure*; this was followed by a number of other books, which consolidate its conclusions as well as advancing into new territory.[10] *The Supreme Adventure* devotes itself to tackling a single relatively manageable question; what, if one regards in the light of travellers' tales the data which appear to be available on the matter from various types of sources, seems to be the experience of the spiritually, morally and intellectually average person shortly after her bodily death? As Crookall remarks, the *opinions* of the immediately dead on religious, spiritual and other matters are apparently just as divided as those of embodied people, and there is no good reason to take those opinions with special seriousness. But the *experiences* which they appear to report are a different matter. One of the most striking results of Crookall's inquiry is the very different kind of experience which is consistently reported as had by those who undergo natural deaths on the one hand, from those who die by violence on the other; people who perish as a result of explosion seem to constitute yet a third category. Those who die natural deaths tend to be comatose for about three days afterwards; after that, they come to full consciousness in an environment corresponding to what has usually been thought of as 'paradise'. Those who die by violence often do not know immediately afterwards that they are dead, and may try ineffectually for a while to attract the attention of those who are still alive; after a while they are contacted by either dead relatives or those who are specialists in this kind of work, who help them to adjust to their new environment.

I do not want to harp on the actual results of Crookall's investigations, which will seem fantastic to those who have not read his book or followed its argument; what has to be emphasized in the present context is the consistency of these results and the method by which Crookall obtains them. His sources are of a nature which have been largely neglected by serious investigators;[11] 'communications' through mediums, 'automatic writing', deathbed visions both by the dying and by those who care for them, the reports of 'clairvoyants' and 'astral travellers', and so on. It is to be remarked that the consensus of recent near-death experiences strongly corroborates Crookall's conclusions, for all that its sources are on the whole of a rather different nature.[12] Apparently, for a number of reasons, those who are farther 'advanced' on the other side are usually either unable or unwilling to communicate through mediums or automatic writing; but according to the psychical researcher G. N. M. Tyrrell, such advanced spirits as do communicate are definitely Christian.[13]

The fact that so much of Crookall's source-material comes through mediums may alarm some readers. But, as Crookall says, it is one thing to subject the phenomena which mediums produce to rational scrutiny; quite another to consider it wise to consult them indiscriminately out of superficial curiosity or in circumstances of personal bereavement. And though Crookall's conclusions seem in overall agreement with what one might suppose if Christianity were true, it is to be noted that many pious opinions are by no means corroborated. The doctrine of many Protestants, that we are to expect no kind of post-mortem existence until the general resurrection, is quite incompatible with his data; so is the popular Christian view that we may expect to see Jesus immediately after our deaths. On the other hand, the practice of praying for the dead, which is commended by some Christians while being disapproved of by others, finds very strong support in his work; one appendix to *The Supreme Adventure*[14] is devoted to appeals by the immediately dead for prayers on their behalf by the living.

Many readers will be strongly disposed, of course, to dismiss Crookall's conclusions out of hand. There is no doubt that they fly in the face of 'common sense' and what are usually thought to be the implications of the scientific worldview. But just the same applied, of course, to the work of the seventeenth-century pioneers of physics and astronomy, whose views notoriously provoked ridicule and resentment among many of their contemporaries. And the sceptic may, I think, not unfairly be asked how she herself would account for what is to be found in the material amassed by Crookall, from sources which are apparently largely independent of one another, but which yield a remarkably consistent picture of what is to be expected by the 'soul', or 'discarnate person', in the time shortly after bodily death. Crookall is quite aware of the objection that his witnesses may all have been affected by a 'mediumistic climate of thought'.[15] But he cites a large number of sources—such as young children and members of 'primitive' cultures[16]—who cannot easily be supposed to have been affected by such a 'climate of thought'. And a number of striking patterns which emerge from the data—especially the differences between the post-mortem experiences of those who die naturally and those who undergo enforced deaths—had never been noticed, so far as I am aware, until this was done by Crookall himself. He claims that there is no case where those who died a natural death are supposed to have communicated through mediums in the first few days after their deaths; which obviously consorts well with the claim that they are in a state of coma during this time.

What is to be said, in the light of all this material and of our previous discussion, of the philosophical objections which have been raised against belief in an afterlife? It seems perfectly easy to conceive of circumstances in which it would appear the most natural thing to say 'So-and-so, who died recently, is trying to communicate with us'; or to imagine what it would be like to be such a being and in similar circumstances oneself. Even if it were granted that Crookall's books or his sources were sheer fiction, they would still abundantly illustrate the point. And that being, or encountering the effects of, such a 'discarnate person' or 'disembodied soul' is so plainly imaginable, seems to militate rather strongly against it being logically impossible. Our usual assumptions about personal identity, to be sure, are based on the circumstances of human life as we ordinarily know it, which are such that a person cannot properly speaking be said to 'remember X', whatever her subjective impressions as though of remembering X, unless she was physically present when and where X took place. But I believe that this is largely because what seem like memories of having witnessed events X or Y, or having had experiences A or B, when one's body was not present on the relevant occasions, and when one has had no ordinary way of acquiring information about the events or experiences in question, are on our usual reckoning so exceptional as to be best explained by appeal to coincidence.

Let us call impressions as though of remembering something, when one prescinds from the question of whether such remembering is genuine or not, 'quasi-memories'. Now let us suppose that such quasi-memories of having been human persons, and having undergone experiences, in far-away places and at times centuries before one's own, became quite commonplace; and that these quasi-memories often checked out as being truthful, even when there were no remotely plausible means that we would now regard as normal by which the subject of the quasi-memories could have acquired the relevant information. Let us further suppose that the recovery of some such quasi-memories was intensely significant for the subject, making a profound difference to her health and her destiny, in much the same manner as some recovered memories of the present life may be significant, as we have come to realize since the work of Sigmund Freud.[17] Would it not then seem the most natural thing to say, that the present subject of these quasi-memories had been the earlier person concerned, or at least that her 'soul' had inhabited a body which together with her 'soul' had constituted that person? Such possibilities seem to make some sense of the doctrine of the resurrection of the body, or the reconstitution of the person.

It appears that there is a great deal of empirical evidence which, when taken together rather than criticized piecemeal,[18] can hardly be understood otherwise than as giving rather strong support for the thesis that, whether we like it or not (and why should all of us be particularly glad at the prospect?), we are to expect some form of life after death. The claims of some older schools of philosophy, to the effect that the 'soul', or thinking and willing aspect of human beings, is not so dependent on the body as necessarily to cease to exist at the latter's death and dissolution, are more firmly based than is often supposed; and the arguments of many of their modern counterparts, to the effect that the view that human beings can expect any form of afterlife is logically incoherent, can be rebutted. I conclude that, though it is true that traditional Christianity entails that we are to enjoy or endure some form at least of life after death, this is no good reason for rejecting it.

Notes

1 For these objections, see especially Part II of A. G. N. Flew, *God, Freedom and Immortality* (Buffalo, NY, 1984).

2 Augustine, *De. Mor. Eccl.* 1, 27, 52; *In Jo. Ev.* 19, 15, 18.

3 Cf. J. A. C. Brown, *Freud and the Post-Freudians* (Harmondsworth, 1961), p. 2.

4 There have been many ingenious attempts by modern philosophers to show how the mental can after all be accounted for exhaustively in terms of the physical. For a very useful account of recent moves in this direction, see William Lyons, 'Modern work on intentionality' in *Faith, Scepticism and Personal Identity: Essays in Honour of Terence Penelhum*, ed. J. J. MacIntosh and H. A. Meynell (Calgary, Alberta, 1994).

5 E. R. Dodds, 'Why I do not believe in survival', *Proceedings of the Society for Psychical Research* (1934); cited by Flew, op. cit., p. 118.

6 Cf. Raymond Moody, *Life After Life* (New York, 1975); *Reflections on Life After Life* (New York, 1977); M. Rawlings, *Beyond Death's Door* (Nashville, TN, 1978).

7 See Gerd H. Hövelmann, 'Evidence for survival from near-death experiences? A critical appraisal' in *A Skeptic's Handbook of Parapsychology*, ed. Paul Kurtz (Buffalo, NY, 1985).

8 Cf. Hövelmann, op. cit., p. 661: '. . . those who were still capable of telling the tale and having their experiences recorded, by definition, cannot have been dead and therefore cannot have had an experience of death.'

9 Cited by R. Crookall, *The Supreme Adventure* (Cambridge, England, 1974), p. 75. I will always be grateful to the late Brother Dunstan Jones CR for having introduced me to this book and suggested its importance.

10 R. Crookall, *The Next World—and the Next* (London, 1966); *What Happens When You Die* (Gerrards Cross, England, 1978).

11 This is a pattern which is worth noting in the advance of human knowledge. No one had much use for

pitchblende, until Marie Curie hit on it as a source of radium.

12 The material is clearly arranged in accordance with its different sources in *The Next World—And the Next*, chapters 5 – 7. Experiences in the case of 'temporary release' are conveniently compared with those in the case of 'permanent release' in *What Happens When You Die*, p. 172.

13 G. N. M. Tyrrell, *Grades of Significance* (London, 1930); cited by Crookall, *The Supreme Adventure*, pp. 231–2.

14 Ibid., Appendix IV.

15 Ibid., pp. 193–6.

16 Ibid., pp. 191–2.

17 Evidence that such strange possibilities are actually the case is presented by Joel L. Whitton, *Life Between Life* (Garden City, NY, 1986). For reincarnation in general, see Hans Ten Dam, *Concerning Reincarnation* (London, 1990).

18 In this connection, a remark of the philosopher F. C. S. Schiller seems worth quoting: 'The man who announces his intention of waiting until a single conclusive bit of evidence turns up is really not open to conviction . . . Single facts can never be "proved" except by their coherence in a system: but, as all facts come singly, anyone who dismisses them one by one is destroying the conditions under which the conviction of new truth could ever arise in his mind': cited by Crookall, *What Happens When You Die*, p. xii.

SEVEN

Conclusion

I have briefly covered quite a number of topics in this little book, and it may be as well to summarize its overall drift. If there is a God, is there any reason to suppose that Christianity is true? It could hardly be true, if it went against the natural human moral conscience. But it was argued that the effect of Christianity, when properly understood and applied, is rather to release and to fortify than to suppress or replace our natural moral intuitions and reasonings. And what applies to morality applies to religion; Christianity could hardly commend itself to reasonable people if it simply contradicted the religious wisdom of the ages. However, Christian doctrines may very plausibly be maintained to be the fulfilment and consummation of the doctrines of the other great religions. Yet this by no means entails that Christians do not have an enormous amount to learn, about how to live, about God and indeed about Christ, from other religious and anti-religious traditions. The doctrine of the person of Christ, set out in dramatic and pictorial terms (the gospels) as well as in a rather more theoretical way (Paul and John) in the New Testament, and successively clarified by the work of the early Christian Fathers and Church Councils, cannot properly be said to be falsified, for all that it *might* well have been so, by the latest and most well-informed historical studies. The doctrine of the Trinity, the central mystery of Christianity, has important bearings on contemporary studies of human consciousness, which in turn clarify it and make it more convincing. The triune God, according to one school of theologians, is absolutely just conception (Son) arising from unrestricted understanding (Father), and infinite love arising from both (Holy Spirit); God is thus both model and goal of human consciousness at its best. The atonement answers human need, as scrutinized through a number of recent types of study. The doctrine of life after death makes sense; and there is now a considerable body of evidence that it is true, quite apart from the fact that it is a clear implication of Christian doctrine.

Ernest Gellner writes as follows:

> *If you insist that a believer specifies the conditions in which his faith would cease to be true, you implicitly force him to conceive a world in which his faith is* sub judice, *at the mercy of some 'fact' or other. But this is precisely what faiths, total outlooks, systematically avoid and evade.*[1]

I should say that no educated person ought to have as a 'faith', or 'total outlook', in the sense implicit in this quotation, anything other than the principle that one should be as reasonable and responsible as possible in one's thinking, speech and behaviour. But I do not think that Christianity is, or need be, a 'faith' or 'total outlook' in quite this sense. I have tried to show that it is reasonable and responsible to believe in the central doctrines of Christianity, when one takes into account the relevant historical studies, basic principles of morality, and the other great religions of humankind. Inquiry into such matters *might have* been subversive of Christianity; but as a matter of fact, as I have argued, it *is* not so.

Note

1   E. Gellner, *The Legitimation of Belief* (London, 1974), p. 174.

APPENDIX A
On Marx on religion

It may be held that one of the main reasons why the religious apologist must be wasting her breath is that Karl Marx has once and for all expounded the nature of religion and exposed its pretensions. In what follows I shall summarize Marx's account of the nature and function of religion, amplify and illustrate this by more detailed reference to his writings, and offer a brief appreciation and criticism.

According to Marx, human beings are naturally cooperative, disposed to work for the overall happiness and fulfilment of other human beings, as well as of themselves. The development of civilization has led to a division of labour, and a corresponding division of people into groups with different and competing interests; accordingly the more powerful groups have tended to maintain their own interests at the expense of the less powerful. As the oppressing groups have increased their power, the misery of the oppressed groups has intensified in proportion; and this process has reached its most extreme possible development in modern industrial society. Religion acts as an analgesic drug for the oppressed members of society, rendering tolerable by fantastic promises for the next world a life which is objectively intolerable in this one. The development of human thought in philosophy and the sciences has already shown that religious

131

beliefs are false; what is now necessary is to reform political and social institutions in such a way that there will no longer be any need for people to use religion as a drug. For technology has now advanced to such an extent that there are enough of the world's goods for all, and that there need no longer be a division of labour; thus after the class divisions which disfigure society have been swept away, each person can spontaneously act for the good of all, and all for the good of each. Then the real satisfaction of human beings in the material world and in each other will make wholly unnecessary the illusory satisfactions of religion, whose real basis in the real oppression of persons by one another and by the forces of nature will have been dispelled respectively by social revolution and by technology.

The theoretical criticism of religion, says Marx, is now complete. Human beings have looked for a superhuman in the heavens, and have found there nothing but a reflection of themselves.[1] Religious persons are apt to declare that philosophy and the sciences do not contradict Christianity. However, it may be noted that there is hardly a philosopher of the first rank who has not been accused of atheism by the pious of his time. Those divines who have insisted on the starkest contrast between the spirit of religion on the one hand, and that of free enquiry on the other, would seem to have grasped the essence of the matter, and to have applied their principles the most consistently.[2] One author informs us that science at its best can but benefit Christianity.[3] However, he supports this remarkable claim by saying that 'any research that contradicts Christianity "stops half-way" or "takes a wrong road". Can one make the argument easier for oneself?' And if, from the start, you assume that everything that is in contradiction with your faith is in error, what is there to distinguish your claims from those of the adherent of any other religion?[4] According to any decent conception of scientific research, this determines its own scope and limits, and is not to be dictated to by religion.[5] As to philosophy, this inquires into what is universally true, not just what is 'true for' particular individuals or communities. Thus 'philosophy's metaphysical truths do not know the boundaries of political geography; its political truths know too well where the "boundaries" begin to confuse the illusory horizon of particular world and historical outlooks with the horizon of the human mind'.[6] It was one of Feuerbach's great merits to have exposed the fallacious foundations of the alliance between religion and reason which was characteristic of Hegel's philosophy and theology, and thus to have compelled religion to show itself in its true colours, as demanding faith in despite of reason.[7]

The theoretical justification of religion, then, has now been discredited; but this is not the main point. The religious illusion arises out of a real human need, which can only be met by a change in human institutions. The basis of religious criticism is that human beings make religion, not religion human beings. Religion is the self-consciousness and feeling about themselves of human beings who have either not yet found themselves, or who have already lost themselves.[8] The cause of religion is real distress, and religion at once expresses this distress and is a protest against it. The abolition of the illusory happiness which people find in religion is required for their real happiness. 'The demand to give up the illusions about its (i.e. the people's) condition is the demand to give up a condition which needs illusions'. So it is that the criticism of heavenly 'realities' turns into a criticism of earthly conditions, the criticism of theology into that of politics.[9] For the spiritual production of a people—its political theories, its law, its morality, its metaphysics, and of course its religion—is directly dependent on its material production, and the real social relations based upon this.

We proceed not from what men say, fancy or imagine, nor from men as they are spoken of, thought, fancied, imagined in order to arrive from them at men of flesh and blood; we proceed from really active men and see the development of the ideological reflexes and echoes of their real life-process as proceeding from that life-process.[10]

The sufferings on which the illusions of religion depend used to be due both to the inscrutable powers of nature and to social maladjustments. Now that nature is at least in principle under control as a result of the developments of science and technology, there remain the inequities in society; these are due ultimately to the division of labour. The division of labour 'implies the possibility, nay, the reality, that spiritual and material activity—enjoyment and work, production and consumption—fall to different individuals'.[11] With the revolution that brings to an end the division of labour, human selfishness, intellectual and moral inequality, and crime will all be done away with, since their economic and social root will have been removed. Then at last the mere prehistory of humanity will be succeeded by its history. One can easily see from the teaching of materialism on the original goodness and intellectual equality of human beings, and the omnipotence of experience and habit and hence of education, how readily it leads to socialism and communism. If human beings derive all their knowledge from the world of the senses, this ought to be arranged in such a way that they get used to what is truly human, and so become aware of themselves as human beings. If morality is based, as it should be, on the principle of properly-understood self-interest, 'man's private interest must be made to coincide with the interest of humanity'. Again, 'crime must not be punished in the individual, but the anti-social source of crime must be destroyed, and each man must be given scope for the vital manifestation of his being'.[12]

I think that Marx thought that acknowledgement of the reality of God was of itself degrading to human beings, quite apart from its deplorable social causes and effects. It is significant that, in his doctoral dissertation of 1831, he calls Prometheus 'the noblest of saints and martyrs in the history of philosophy'.[13] Later he was to write that

> *the criticism of religion ends with the teaching that* man is the highest essence for man, *hence with the* categoric imperative to overthrow all relations *in which man is a debased, enslaved, abandoned, despicable essence.*[14]

So much for a brief exegesis of Marx's views on the nature and function of religion. On this subject, as in his thought in general, Marx seems to me to show a remarkable mixture of insight and oversight. I shall argue this thesis in what follows.

His insistence that scientific investigation should assign its own scope and limits, and not have these dictated by some other authority—in particular, by religion—is reasonable in one sense, not in another. It is unreasonable in the sense that the question of the scope and limits of empirical investigation cannot itself be determined by empirical investigation. How could one possibly determine, by appeal to sense-experience, whether or not there are any coherent questions which cannot be settled by appeal to sense-experience, and of what nature these questions are, assuming that there are any such? It is reasonable in the sense that there seem grounds for supposing that any realm of discourse, particularly if it depends for its validity on assertions of real fact and actual existence, should be subjected to a critical investigation which does not itself presuppose the truth of these assertions. It should be asked, firstly, to what extent the realm of discourse is coherent with itself; and secondly, what good reason there is for asserting the truth of the propositions and the reality of the things and states of affairs on which the realm of discourse depends for its validity.[15] For example, Christian theology may be said to presuppose that there is a God, that God is revealed uniquely in Jesus Christ, and that this revelation is conveyed to human beings through the media of Scripture and the Church. One may properly ask whether there are grounds for believing either that God exists, or that God is so revealed. If Marx's requirement is interpreted in this sense, I strongly agree with him, against (for example) Karl Barth and D. Z. Phillips, that religion and Christianity require a justification which is external to themselves.[16] Traditional Roman Catholic teaching acknowledged this when it asserted the necessity for a 'fundamental' theology which was a part of philosophy, and which was presupposed by the dogmatic theologian. In general, it seems to me one of the central tasks of philosophy to investigate the grounds for beliefs of all kinds, whether scientific, or religious, or anything else, and to find out whether the conflicts between scientific and religious beliefs are real or apparent. I do not however agree with Marx or with Kai Nielsen[17] that such an investigation must necessarily lead to atheism.

I cited earlier Marx's aspersions on the work of a certain Christian apologist. It may be seen from what I have said that these are well-grounded or not, according to what the apologist was really doing. If he was assuming *without further argument* that those conclusions of science which contradicted Christian belief were *by that very fact* wrong, then Marx's objections are quite correct. But the apologist may, at least to judge by Marx's quotations from him, only have meant that it was always *as a matter of fact* the case that, when an alleged scientific discovery appeared to contradict Christian belief, either the alleged discovery would be shown to be erroneous by subsequent scientific inquiry, or that the belief contradicted was no essential part of Christianity. An example of the kind of matter which is at issue may be taken from biblical criticism. Some conclusions as to the historical validity of the gospels which have been arrived at by scholars are inconsistent with traditional Christian belief. The kind of attitude to which Marx rightly objects—which is often attributed to conservative evangelicals by radical critics—would make a person reject such conclusions as unscientific *just because* they conflicted with Christian belief. But it does not seem on the face of it wrong in principle to argue—as in fact conservative evangelicals often do—that, on the grounds of scientific investigation itself, certain historical conclusions which would tell heavily against Christianity are themselves based on insufficient evidence or unsound argument. If his opponent might be accused of assuming without question that science and Christian belief must be in harmony with one another, Marx might be accused of being too ready to assume that they are in conflict.

It is central to Marx's thinking that the legal, political and religious ideas of a people are dependent, wholly or at least very largely, on the mode of production and the resulting social relationships prevalent among them. It may be asked whether the same thing applies to scientific ideas. If it does not, it may be asked for what reason this particular class of ideas is exempt. If it does, one looks for a clear criterion according to which scientific doctrines may state what is the case about reality, religious ones not. Marx says that it is basic to the criticism of religion that humanity makes religion, not religion humanity; but humanity also makes science, and this does not of itself show, at least in Marx's view, that science is a bundle of illusions. It might be replied that scientific beliefs concern exclusively what can be seen, touched and so on, whereas religious beliefs do not. Interpreted *au pied de la lettre*, this proposition was false in Marx's time, and is now more obviously so. 'Mass', in the sense defined by Newton's law, is not an observable phenomenon; it is a theoretical construct, the real existence of which in nature is admittedly *verified in* observation. The same applies to such things as electrons and positrons, which as I understand not only *are* not observed, but *could not conceivably* be observed; however, their existence would seem to have observable consequences. To meet this objection, Marx might argue that while many of the things postulated by scientists could not be direct objects of experience, at least the consequences of their existence and presence could be a part of our experience. But the appeal to experience thus relaxed in order to accommodate science would by no means obviously exclude religious belief.[18] Many theists hold that God's existence must be asserted in order to account either for the world-order of our experience as a whole, or for some aspect of it.

Marx's assumption that the rejection of idealism must lead to materialism seems to involve either a misleadingly broad sense given to the term 'materialism', or the neglect of some important possibilities. The essence of 'idealism', I take it, is that what we call 'the real world' is itself in the last analysis the product of our thought, rather than existing, as on the common-sense view, prior to our thought, and determining the truth or falsity of our beliefs by correspondence with itself. But if we label the negation of idealism in the given sense as 'realism', there are at least two forms of realism, only one of which is obviously inconsistent with theism. According to one of these, the real is what is or can be the direct object of sensation—what can be seen, felt and so on. Clearly, this leads directly to atheism, since hardly anyone supposes that God is an actual or possible object of sensation. But this form of realism, as I have already tried to show, makes just as much nonsense of modern science as it does of religious belief. Yet the form of realism which insists merely that real things and properties must be such as to *account for* or *explain* actual or possible experience is not at all obviously incompatible with belief in God.

Having said something about Marx's theoretical objections to religion, I shall now deal with the moral objections which play a more important role in his thinking. On his account remediable social evils both create the need for religious belief, and are maintained in existence with the help of these beliefs. That religion has often been used and is often used to induce people to put up with an unjust social order is certain and by now notorious; it is part of Marx's greatness to have made the point so clearly and forcefully. But religion does seem to have other moral and social functions, including that of encouraging persons to renounce their selfish satisfactions when the pursuit of these runs counter to the interests of society at large.

According to Marx, there would be no dichotomy between individual and general interest in a just society, since human beings are naturally co-operative, and are only forced into selfishness by untoward physical or social circumstances. He is surely right in his opposition to the pessimistic Hobbist and Freudian view that every person naturally seeks the fulfilment only of her own needs and desires, and can be made to co-operate with her fellows only by external constraint. He also has the merit of having brought out with unrivalled trenchancy the manner in which social injustice and material want at least exacerbate whatever tendency there is in individuals and groups to seek their own good in opposition to that of other individuals and groups. But it does not follow from this that human beings have a natural tendency to seek the good of their fellows above all else; or that they would do so as a matter of course even if social institutions were constructed in such a way as to induce them so far as possible to do so. Both the study of actual human behaviour, and reflection on probable human evolution, tell rather heavily against all of the following three views, of which Marx seems to have held a blend of the second and the third: that human beings are naturally selfish; that they are naturally devoted to the general good of their fellows; or that each person is a *tabula rasa* in this respect, open to an indefinite degree of social conditioning. Most human races at least have apparently evolved in rather small groups which survived by competing successfully with other similar groups; and there is plenty of evidence in actual human behaviour that we are genetically programmed to find satisfaction in co-operation with our own group and aggression against others. It looks, in fact, as though dissensions between human individuals and groups were exasperated rather than created by economic and social inequalities; and as though, even in an ideal society, a human being could only come to be committed to the general good as the result of rather arduous self-dedication.

Marxists may object that these alleged limits to the changeability of human behaviour are matters of speculation rather than rigorous proof. But what is sauce for the goose is sauce for the gander. While the evidence for the less optimistic view may not amount to conclusive proof, this by no means implies that the contrary and Marxist view can be taken as certain. What is apt to be taken as evidence for it in fact tells only against the view which is at the opposite extreme, that every human being is by nature selfish. Marx is right to stress that human behaviour is to a large extent affected by the immediate material and social conditions within which we live out our lives; but he does not attend sufficiently to the fact that *homo sapiens* is an animal which has evolved over many millions of years, and that this evolution is liable to impose limits to the malleability of its emotions and its dispositions to behaviour by its immediate circumstances.

Communists may not have any use for the opposition of individual and general interest;[19] but the fact remains that it exists, and that there is evidence that it will exist as long as human beings live in this world. While it exists, religious belief, or some surrogate for it, will always have a role in heartening people in pursuit of the general good even when it goes against their own particular interest. My general conclusion is that, while a great deal is to be learned from Marx's intellectual and moral objections to religious belief, they can be rebutted without serious difficulty.

Notes

All references not otherwise assigned will be to *On Religion: Writings by K. Marx and F. Engels* (Moscow, 1957).

1 *Contribution to the Critique of Hegel's Philosophy of Right* (CHPR), p. 41.
2 *On the Leading Article of No. 179 of Kölnische Zeitung* (KZ), p. 24.
3 KZ, p. 21.
4 KZ, p. 25.
5 KZ, p. 21.
6 KZ, p. 26.
7 *The Holy Family* (HF), p. 62.
8 CHPR, p. 41.
9 CHPR, p. 42.
10 *The German Ideology* (GI), p. 71.
11 GI, pp. 76–7.
12 HF, pp. 67–8.
13 *Philosophy of Democritus and Philosophy of Epicurus*, p. 15.
14 CHPR, p. 50.
15 Cf. L. Wittgenstein, *On Certainty* (New York: J. and J. Harper Editions, 1969), para. 617: 'Doesn't it seem obvious that the possibility of a language-game is conditioned by certain facts?'
16 Cf. Karl Barth, *Church Dogmatics* (Edinburgh, 1936–62), I, 2, pp. 172f.; D. Z. Phillips, *The Concept of Prayer* (London, 1965), p. 10.
17 Cf. Kai Nielsen, 'Language and the concept of God', *Question* (January 1969).
18 The point is well made by W. Pannenberg, *Theology and the Philosophy of Science* (London, 1976), p. 55.
19 *The German Ideology*, ed. C. J. Arthur (London, 1979), p. 104.

APPENDIX B

A philosophical note

It has been objected by an anonymous philosopher, whom for convenience I shall refer to as McF, that this book as a whole is an exercise in 'the fallacy of affirming the consequent'. I do not think that this objection would be made by anyone who was not a professional philosopher; but since it has been made, and since a few of my readers may either be professional philosophers, or be inclined to defer to the authority of such persons, it may be worth devoting a little space to its rebuttal.

'If A then B; A; therefore B' is a valid argument. If the premises are true, you can rely on the conclusion being so. 'If A then B; B; therefore A' is not a valid argument; it involves the fallacy of affirming the consequent. Even if the premises happen to be true, you can by no means rely on the truth of the conclusion. 'If anyone is a Friesian bull, he is male; Julius Caesar is male; therefore Julius Caesar is a Friesian bull' is not a good argument; and, as is apt to be the case with bad arguments, two true premises lead to a false conclusion.

Why should the claim that I have perpetrated the fallacy of affirming the consequent be sufficiently colourable to be alleged by any sane person? The argument of this book might be rather carelessly presented as follows: 'If Christianity is true, Christianity suits the human moral plight, and the gospels are at least roughly historical. But

Christianity suits the human moral plight, and the gospels are at least roughly historical. Therefore Christianity is true.' As it stands, this does indeed involve the fallacy of affirming the consequent.

But something will have occurred to the alert reader to put her on her guard. What is it to find evidence for any claim, say in a scientific experiment, or in a murder investigation? Does not the argument from the evidence to the truth of a theory, or to the guilt or innocence of the accused as charged, in almost any conceivable instance, involve at first sight this very fallacy of affirming the consequent? From the existence of a certain kind of heavenly body, perhaps, together with various physical laws, it follows that in appropriate circumstances recording pencils in a radio-telescope will make marks of a certain shape. But it is only by the fallacy of affirming the consequent, surely, that one can argue from the occurrence of such marks that such a kind of heavenly body exists? The argument, in fact, from the occurrence of any data to the truth of the theory supposed to explain such data may seem at first sight to be vitiated by the same fallacy. Is scientific method as a whole, then, fallacious?

The fact is that another procedure of reasoning, which may easily be confused by the unwary with the fallacy of affirming the consequent, is universal and absolutely indispensable both in science and in the prosecution of ordinary human affairs. This may be called the argument to the best explanation. A puzzling phenomenon turns up; one casts around for possible explanations; and one finally, so far as one is reasonable, fixes provisionally on the explanation which best fits the phenomenon. Water may be a chemical element, or it may be a chemical compound; its being an element, for all that it was believed for millennia, is incompatible with the observable fact that it can be electrolysed into two gases with differing properties. So the reasonable person prefers, as more in accordance with this and a vast range of other evidence, the proposition that water is a chemical compound. 'If water is a chemical compound, it follows that it can be divided into its constituent elements. But it can be divided into its constituent elements. Therefore water is a compound'—that is fallacious, but it seems perilously like the form of argument which scientists do in fact follow. In fact, this form of argument is better represented thus: 'If water were not a chemical compound, it would not be able to be divided into constitutive elements. But water can be divided into constitutive elements. Therefore water is a chemical compound.' This argument has a perfectly valid form: 'If A, then B; not B; therefore not A.'

What it comes to is that McF has confused the normal mode of scientific reasoning, which should be expressed in the valid form which I have just set out, with a well-known logical fallacy. I contend that my own argument, whatever may be its incidental demerits, at least is in conformity with the very general norms of scientific reasoning. *Given* the existence of God, *given* that God might have been expected to do something about the human moral plight, *given* that the putative facts alleged by the gospel writers might reasonably be supposed to constitute this something, and *given* that the approximate historical truth of these narratives may be corroborated in other ways, *then* the truth of Christian doctrine (or some version thereof) may be commended as the best explanation. To put it succinctly, if Christianity were not true, events like those recorded in the gospels would not have happened. But events like those recorded in the gospels have happened. Therefore Christianity is true. Whatever view one may have of the truth of either of the premises or of the conclusion of this argument, it is a valid one, in the technical sense that the conclusion does follow from the premises. The kind of evidence by which one might support the premises is just what I have been concerned to adduce throughout this little book.

A final brief point seems worth making about the ethics of controversy; this may be generally applied to the discussion of religious and political issues, where feelings tend to run high. Suppose two possible interpretations of what one's opponent has said suggest themselves; in accordance with one of which she can be dismissed without more ado as an ignorant fool or an arrant knave; in accordance with the other of which there may be some grounds for taking her seriously. A conscientious person, who is at least as interested in finding out the truth as in appearing to score points against ideological opponents, will be inclined to attend to and pause over the second possible interpretation, rather than fixing immediately and gleefully upon the first. Particularly where religious and political issues are in question, we have had a great deal too much of this sort of intellectual sharp practice. McF would do well to take the point to heart.

Index

Index

148

Index